# Live Lent!

## Year A

By *Theresa Rickard, O.P.*

D1411825

RENEW International gratefully acknowledges contributors to this work: Martin Lang and Trish Sullivan Vanni.

NIHIL OBSTAT
    Dianne Traflet, J.D., S.T.D.
    Censor Librorum

IMPRIMATUR
    Most Reverend John J. Myers, J.C.D., D.D.
    Archbishop of Newark

Cover design by Ruth Markworth
Interior Design Consultant: Blue Willow Publishing Works
Interior Page Layout by Clara Baumann
Cover photo © Radu Razvan Gheorghe | Dreamstime.com

ISBN: 978-1-62063-122-5

RENEW International
    1232 George Street
    Plainfield, NJ 07062-1717
    www.renewintl.org

Printed and bound in the United States of America

# Contents

Live Lent! . . . . . . . . . . . . . . . . . . . . . . . . . . . . . . . . . . . . . . . . . . . . . . . . . . 4

Your Lenten Plan: 40 Days to Live Lent! . . . . . . . . . . . . . . . . . . . . . . . . . 8

Daily Meditations: Ash Wednesday . . . . . . . . . . . . . . . . . . . . . . . . . . . . 10

First Sunday of Lent . . . . . . . . . . . . . . . . . . . . . . . . . . . . . . . . . . . . . . . . 15

Daily Meditations: First Week of Lent . . . . . . . . . . . . . . . . . . . . . . . . . 21

Second Sunday of Lent . . . . . . . . . . . . . . . . . . . . . . . . . . . . . . . . . . . . . 28

Daily Meditations: Second Week of Lent . . . . . . . . . . . . . . . . . . . . . . . 34

Third Sunday of Lent . . . . . . . . . . . . . . . . . . . . . . . . . . . . . . . . . . . . . . . 42

Daily Meditations: Third Week of Lent . . . . . . . . . . . . . . . . . . . . . . . . . 49

Fourth Sunday of Lent . . . . . . . . . . . . . . . . . . . . . . . . . . . . . . . . . . . . . . 57

Daily Meditations: Fourth Week of Lent . . . . . . . . . . . . . . . . . . . . . . . . 64

Fifth Sunday of Lent . . . . . . . . . . . . . . . . . . . . . . . . . . . . . . . . . . . . . . . . 72

Daily Meditations: Fifth Week of Lent . . . . . . . . . . . . . . . . . . . . . . . . . 80

Palm Sunday of the Passion of the Lord . . . . . . . . . . . . . . . . . . . . . . . 88

Daily Meditations: Holy Week . . . . . . . . . . . . . . . . . . . . . . . . . . . . . . . . 96

Easter Sunday . . . . . . . . . . . . . . . . . . . . . . . . . . . . . . . . . . . . . . . . . . . . 104

Appendix: Feast Days and Solemnities . . . . . . . . . . . . . . . . . . . . . . . 106

About the Author . . . . . . . . . . . . . . . . . . . . . . . . . . . . . . . . . . . . . . . . . . 111

Presenting RENEW International . . . . . . . . . . . . . . . . . . . . . . . . . . . . . 112

The Structure and Flow of a Session . . . . . . . . . . . . . . . . . . . . . . . . . 113

Additional Resources from RENEW International . . . . . . . . . . . . . . . 115

# LIVE LENT!

Theresa Rickard, O.P.

**At one summer** barbecue with friends and family, a neighbor sat down to chat with me. It was generally known that he was "anti-religion." Although I had met him a few times, we had never had a real conversation. People like him either avoid me completely, because I'm "the nun," or they seek me out for the same reason. He began to share with me about his childhood in a very strict Christian Church. There was no drinking, women wore very modest attire, and there was no openness to other religions or their adherents. He found the faithful in his family's church harsh, cold, and judgmental. As soon as he was old enough, he left his church and his Christian faith and did not look back. His wife is agnostic, and they chose not to raise their children in any faith tradition. They're both good people—altruistic, reflective, and highly ethical—and, after all these years, they seem to be seeking God, or at least a higher being.

He told me, as I've heard many times before, that the people in his church experience did not live faith; it was all about the rules, giving up worldly things, and the fear of hell and damnation. This description of a Christian community is so opposed to the biblical view of the movement that Jesus initiated! How do good, well-intentioned religious people get so far from authentic Christian worship and living? It is the human thing to become self-righteous and judgmental, not the God thing. I tried to just listen and not become defensive—which is not easy for me. I obviously believe organized religion is essential, but I also know all churches including the Catholic Church, sometimes fall short of Jesus' vision. I, too, am angered and frustrated by the way we sometimes fail God's people and ultimately fail God when we are merciless and unwelcoming. Pope Francis exhorts us over and over again to be a Church that is merciful, listening, and accepting—to meet people "where they're at."

The ongoing challenge for all of us is to live faith and to embrace the call from Jesus to love God and neighbor. Lent is an opportunity to spend 40 days focused on becoming more authentic lovers of God and followers of Christ—to live Lent with the resolve to make real change in our lives. This year, we strive to Live Lent! so we can live faith more authentically each and every day—to make God real and present in our hurting world through our loving actions.

## Preparing for Lent

For me, the Lenten season has always been a time to refocus on God and get my life in right order. I want to Live Lent! so I can live faith with greater integrity and in deeper communion with God and my neighbor. As a child I thought Lent was about giving up things like candy and fighting with my sister, Mary. I have come to realize that it is not so much about giving up things but about seizing the opportunity to be all that God has called me to be—a holy, healthy, and loving person—a disciple of Jesus Christ committed to transforming my faith into real-life action.

**So, let me suggest not ways to fast but things to do and things not to do this Lent. First, things to do:**

**Consciously surrender to God.** Whenever we say the Lord's Prayer we ask that God's will be done on earth. And Lent reminds us that leading a Christian life means setting aside our will—our desires and wishes and priorities—and asking God to help us behave only according to God's will.

**Let go of old self-images.** Imitating Jesus, who died on the cross, is to empty ourselves of ego and see ourselves as who we really are—creatures totally dependent on our Creator, but also living reflections of God's love and compassion. We are flawed and fabulous, and we need to let go of denigrating ourselves and old tapes that tell us that we are not good enough or smart enough or attractive enough. Lent is a time to see ourselves clearly—as Father Richard Rohr's says, to find our true selves, our God selves, our Christ selves.

**Focus on engendering life from within.** No matter what we own or what we lack in the way of material possessions or wealth, our greatest gifts to each other, to the world at large, will always come from within us. Be conscious of the Holy Spirit encouraging your powers of love, compassion, and justice; realize the potential in these gifts; find ways to use these gifts to bless the lives of others in large ways and small.

**Ask for the grace of transformation.** Pray each day that you will emerge from this Lenten experience as a new person. Leave the details of your renewal up to God, and thank God for this grace.

## And now, things not to do:

**Don't give up.** Instead of giving up something for Lent, try doing something that will bring you closer to God. Perhaps attend Mass during the week, spend time reflecting on the daily or Sunday readings by yourself and with others by using this book, experience the beauty of God's creation by taking walks, make donations to your favorite charities, volunteer at the local food bank, light candles and say prayers for the people you know who are struggling. If you still decide to give something up, do it for someone else. For example, if you give up wine for Lent, each time you decline to take wine, pray for someone who struggles with an addiction to alcohol.

**Don't sweat it.** Whatever it is you commit to do this Lent, the point isn't to do it perfectly. Give it your best, but if you slip up, accept that as a reminder that you are not perfect. Only God is perfect. Say a prayer, and start again.

**Don't starve yourself.** Lent isn't about going on a diet or losing weight—it's about the conversion of hearts. Eat healthy, get some exercise, but don't succumb to our culture's obsession with physical appearances. Again, if you want to give up sweets, do it while praying for someone who is seriously overweight.

**Don't make it more difficult than it is.** The three pillars of Lent are prayer, fasting, and almsgiving. Find simple ways to pray, fast, and give to those who live in poverty.

**Don't hold back.** Lent will present you with many opportunities to convert your heart and your life, to heal broken relationships, and to grow closer to God. When you find yourself presented with such an opportunity, embrace it.

So this Lent don't give up, don't sweat it, don't starve yourself, don't make it more difficult than it is, and, most especially, don't hold back! Live Lent! so you can live a more authentic faith long after these 40 days have passed.

# 40 Days to Live Lent!

**A good Lent** begins with a plan. Just as we carefully plan for big events in our personal lives, such as a graduation or a wedding, Lent invites us to make our hearts ready for remembering Jesus' passion and celebrating Jesus' resurrection. The best way to celebrate Jesus' resurrection is to live more fully Christ's life in the here and now.

What are some actions this Lent that can deepen your relationship with God, make you more aware of God's presence in your life, and help you to be kinder, more loving, to others? Reflect on your life and where you are in your relationship with God. Which relationship in your life most needs forgiveness and God's healing presence? What are you doing for people who are poor and needy? What bad habit is keeping you away from God? What do you need to change?

Pray about it; ask God. We can't make changes in our lives without God's grace. Willpower is never enough. Now, write down simple actions under each of the three areas we are invited to act on during Lent: prayer, fasting, and almsgiving (giving to those in need and supporting our parish and other worthy organizations). Many parishes participate in CRS Rice Bowl through which millions of Catholics in the United States apply the Lenten pillars of praying, fasting, and almsgiving to help alleviate hunger around the world. See if your parish does this, or help to establish the program in your parish. For more information, go to www.crsricebowl.org.

Remember, we are called to live Lent so we can live faith not only during these 40 days but every day henceforth.

Jot down the commitments you will make in each of these areas. Remember, keep it simple and doable. Review your Lenten commitments each Sunday during Lent, and make adjustments. Don't give up; keep at it.

**Prayer:**

_____

_____

_____

_____

_____

_____

_____

_____

**Fasting:**

_____

_____

_____

_____

_____

_____

_____

_____

**Almsgiving:**

_____

_____

_____

_____

_____

_____

_____

_____

## Ash Wednesday

 **Pray**

*"Be merciful, O Lord, for we have sinned." (Psalm 51:3a)*

 **Read** *Joel 2:12-18*

**Summary:**    *"Even now, says the Lord, return to me with your whole heart, with fasting, and weeping, and mourning; Rend your hearts, not your garments, and return to the Lord, your God.... Blow the trumpet in Zion! proclaim a fast, call an assembly; Gather the people, notify the congregation" (Joel 2:12-13, 15-16)*

*Spend two minutes in silence. Then repeat this passage from Scripture and let it speak to your heart.*

 **Meditation**

Today we officially begin our 40-day Lenten journey. The first reading from the prophet Joel from today's Mass is the heart of our Lenten call: return to God with our whole hearts! Being smudged with ashes, marked with the sign of the cross, is a visible sign to us and all we meet today of our commitment to say yes to the prophet's clarion call to conversion of heart. The symbol of ashes reminds us that we are dust and that it is through the breath of God that we have been given life. This is not a curse but what it means to be a vulnerable human being who finds life and purpose by following God's grand plan—to be our best selves for God! Ashes also can remind us that what we touch turns to dust if we have not acted in God's name and out of love for another.

We commit ourselves during Lent to increase our giving to those who are poor, to prayer, and to fasting—not to impress others but to bear witness to our belief in Jesus Christ and his call to love God with all our hearts and our neighbor as ourselves. Remember that means to share love with even those who are most annoying and those who don't earn or appreciate our love.

# Live Lent!

I will spend time today reflecting on what it means to wear a cross of ashes on my forehead. If at all possible, I will share my thoughts with someone else.

 **Pray**

*Lord Jesus, give me the courage to witness to my faith in gentle and respectful ways. I pray for the grace to devote my whole heart to you through the power of the Holy Spirit. Amen.*

## Thursday after Ash Wednesday

 **Pray**

*"Choose life, then, that you and your descendants may live, by loving the Lord, your God, heeding his voice, and holding fast to him." (Deuteronomy 30:19b-20)*

 **Read** *Luke 9:22-25*

**Summary:**   *"If anyone wishes to come after me, he must deny himself and take up his cross daily and follow me. For whoever wishes to save his life will lose it, but whoever loses his life for my sake will save it." (Luke 9:23b-24)*

*Spend two minutes in silence. Then repeat this passage from Scripture and let it speak to your heart.*

 **Meditation**

Jesus revealed true love by losing his life so that we may experience fullness of life now and in eternity. Lent is an opportunity to examine our lives in light of our decision to be followers of Christ. The cost of discipleship is losing ourselves in Christ's love so we may find our truest selves in loving others. It is the cross of sacrificial love that we choose to carry daily. It is the only path to life.

# Live Lent!

Without complaint or resentment, I will do an ordinary act of love that has some personal cost to me.

 **Pray**

*Lord Jesus, give me the grace to lose myself in you, so I can become a more loving person. Help me choose each day to do the loving thing, no matter what it costs me, and so come to know abundant life in you. Amen.*

## Friday after Ash Wednesday

 **Pray**

*"This, rather, is the fasting that I wish: releasing those bound unjustly, untying the thongs of the yoke; Setting free the oppressed, breaking every yoke; Sharing your bread with the hungry, sheltering the oppressed and the homeless; Clothing the naked when you see them...."* (Isaiah 58:6-7a)

 **Read** *Matthew 9:14-15*

**Summary:** *"The disciples of John approached Jesus and said, 'Why do we and the Pharisees fast much, but your disciples do not fast?'"* Matthew 9:14

*Spend two minutes in silence. Then repeat this passage from Scripture and let it speak to your heart.*

**Meditation**

Fasting is a beneficial spiritual practice anytime. It is especially helpful during Lent as we prepare for Easter. True fasting, devoted to prayer and charity, can transform us. The purpose of fasting is to help control our unruly selves for the sake of purifying our hearts and growing our capacity to practice charity. Fasting can help us surrender to God food or whatever else has power over us. It can help us let go of our compulsions and distractions so that these habits and material things can return to their rightful places in our lives. The fasting that Isaiah calls us to in today's first reading drives us from a life of selfishness or habit-driven living to one of generous giving and self-control.

## Live Lent!

I will carefully consider what I have chosen to give up for Lent and determine how the void created by my fast can be filled with what comes from God.

 **Pray**

*Lord Jesus, your Word is the only food that will satisfy my hungry heart. Give me your grace to enter into a true fast this Lent. Through prayer and fasting, may my unruly self be refocused on your will and way. Help me to grow in my willingness to practice charity. Amen.*

## Saturday after Ash Wednesday

 **Pray**

*"He will renew your strength, and you shall be like a watered garden, like a spring whose water never fails."* (Isaiah 58:11b)

 **Read** *Luke 5:27-32*

**Summary:** *"'Why do you eat and drink with tax collectors and*

sinners?' Jesus said to them in reply, 'Those who are healthy do not need a physician, but the sick do. I have not come to call the righteous to repentance but sinners.'" *(Luke 5:30b-32)*

*Spend two minutes in silence. Then repeat this passage from Scripture and let it speak to your heart.*

 **Meditation**

This brief gospel scene is compelling because it describes not just Jesus calling one disciple, but his call to every person. Jesus moved through Galilean society, not handpicking the smartest and the purest but instead the castoffs. The scandal of this scene in the eyes of the religious was that Jesus called forth a new community of disciples based on association with sinners rather than separation from them. Levi responds to Jesus' call in two ways: first, he leaves everything behind and follows Jesus; second, he throws a party for Jesus, a party crowded with tax collectors. He does not give up on his friends but instead draws them into the presence of Christ.

# *Live Lent!*

I will reach out in kindness to someone who seems to be lonely, hurting, or despairing.

 **Pray**

*Lord Jesus, transform me by the power of your Spirit, so I may become your compassionate and welcoming presence to all. Renew your Church so we may become a true home for those who are unwanted, or lost, or unacceptable. Amen.*

*"The Lord ... alone shall you serve"*

## Suggested Environment

A small table with a burning candle and a Bible opened to the gospel reading for this session. Consider decorating the table with violet, the liturgical color of the Lenten season. Place a bowl containing sand on the table.

### *Liturgical Readings for the*
### *First Sunday of Lent*

GENESIS 2:7-9; 3:1-7
*Adam and Eve give in to temptation.*

PSALM 51:3-4, 5-6, 12-14, 17
*"Be merciful, O Lord for we have sinned."*

ROMANS 5:12-19
*"Through one righteous act, acquittal and life came to all."*

MATTHEW 4:1-11
*"You shall not put the Lord, your God, to the test."*

## Focus

In the "wilderness times" of our lives, our recourse is to God.

**Opening Song** (To download, visit ocp.org/renew-music.)

"*Create in Me,*" Bob Hurd, Anawim, or "*Loving and Forgiving,*" Scott Soper

 **Opening Prayer**

*Form two groups, and pray alternately from Psalm 51, with everyone repeating the response:*

**R.**　　　**Be merciful, O Lord, for we have sinned.**

**Side 1:**　Have mercy on me, O God in your goodness;
　　　　　　in the greatness of your compassion wipe
　　　　　　out my offense.
　　　　　　Thoroughly wash me from my guilt
　　　　　　and of my sin cleanse me.

**R.**　　　**Be merciful, O Lord, for we have sinned.**

**Side 2:**　For I acknowledge my offense,
　　　　　　and my sin is before me always.
　　　　　　"Against you only have I sinned,
　　　　　　and done what is evil in your sight."

**R.**　　　**Be merciful, O Lord, for we have sinned.**

**Side 1:**　A clean heart create for me, O God;
　　　　　　a steadfast spirit renew within me.
　　　　　　Cast me not out from your presence,
　　　　　　and your Holy Spirit take not from me.

**R.**　　　**Be merciful, O Lord, for we have sinned.**

**Side 2:**　Give me back the joy of your salvation,
　　　　　　and a willing spirit sustain in me.
　　　　　　O Lord, open my lips,
　　　　　　and my mouth shall proclaim your praise.

**R:**　　　**Be merciful, O Lord, for we have sinned.**

**The Gospel of the Lord**

*"One does not live on bread alone, but on every word that comes forth from the mouth of God." (Matthew 4:4b)*

**Read** *aloud* Matthew 4:1–11

## Reflect

*What word, phrase, or image from the scripture reading touches your heart or connects to your experience? Share with the group, and/or write your response here:*

_____

_____

_____

_____

## Old Testament Connections

The ancient Israelites, wandering in the parched desert and following Moses, were tempted severely. They complained, asking why he had led them to such a barren place where there was no food. (Ex 16:3). Had Moses led them astray, or was their protector God no longer with them? But the Lord heard their cries and sent quail in the evening and the sweet bread-like substance called manna in the morning.

The words of Jesus in the passage about his own time in the desert, echo the teachings and the conduct of Moses. It is clear that Jesus does not supplant Moses in the tradition. In fact, in repeating the core of Moses' teaching—"The Lord your God shall you fear; him shall you serve" (Dt 6:13)—Jesus brings a new clarity, a fresh understanding to Moses' words. In the Gospel of Matthew, there are clarifications, about the Sabbath, about fasting, and about the gentiles from the new Moses, but the authority of Moses remains intact.

The great challenge to Israel's faith as described in Moses' last words to his followers was to not give in to temptation, to not yield to the values of the Canaanite people who believed their fertility gods caused the crops to grow (Dt 31:16-29). For Israel's nomadic herders who were integrating into a Canaanite agricultural lifestyle, the temptation was to accept the gods of the successful farmers. It is a marvel that, throughout their integration into an agrarian society, the Israelites preserved at all their faith in a Leader-God. But that success was due to the contribution of the prophets, and particularly of Elijah who confronted and challenged the Israelite king Ahab and his wife, Jezebel, who had bought the entire package from the Canaanites (1 Kgs 18).

Significantly, the temptation of Jesus takes place immediately after he was baptized by John, who appeared in the wilderness, in his rough garments, like the prophet Elijah (2 Kg 1:8), and called for repentance. Elijah disappeared into the heavens (2 Kgs 2:11) giving rise to the tradition that he would return before the coming of the iconic, faithful king of Israel, the new David, the Messiah. Now here is John, Elijah-like, proclaiming the coming kingdom of God. John's words have the same urgency concerning repentance as do those of Amos when he proclaims the day of the Lord as "darkness not light" (Am 5:18). John's words also specifically repeat Isaiah's famous call, "Prepare the way of the Lord" (Is 40:3).

*Adapted from a reflection by Martin Lang in* Matthew: Come Follow Me, *part of the* RENEW Scripture Series.

## Reflect

*The modern world presents its own temptations that can distract us from living as disciples of Jesus. What distractions do you encounter, and how do you deal with them? Share with the group, and/or write your response here.*

---

---

---

---

 **Meditate**

Shortly after my dad died, my mom said to me, "Sometimes I look around this house, in which I have lived for more than 30 years, and I don't know where I am. I feel homeless." The loss of a loved one is one of life's crises that can throw us into a kind of wilderness experience that may breed disorientation, loneliness, and vulnerability. A few weeks later my mom remarked, "I don't know if I have the desire or the energy to begin a new life."

A wilderness journey is a time of testing, but also an opportunity to choose life in the midst of impending despair, or to opt for God's way instead of the shallowness of immediate gratification. It is a time that takes advantage of our human weakness and opens us to temptation. But it also can be a time for growth.

We begin Lent by reading about the temptation of Jesus in the wilderness. He didn't choose the wilderness but instead was led there by the Spirit. When the community Matthew was writing for heard about 40 days in the wilderness they immediately recalled the Exodus event. For the Israelites, the desert was not a success story—they failed the test and turned their backs on God. However, God remained faithful to them.

Wilderness times test our faith, too, and challenge us to be transformed. My mom, through God's grace, eventually emerged from the desolation of grief. God sent angels to minister to her. God will do the same for you.

## Reflect

*When has an experience of loss or disappointment tested your faith?*

_____

_____

_____

_____

*What resources are available to you—in the Church, in your personal relationships, and in your interior life—that could help you maintain your faith if you have another such experience?*

_____

_____

_____

_____

*How can you be an "angel" to those who experience loss?*

_____

_____

_____

_____

# Live Lent!

✝ Recall a time God led you through a wilderness time. Who was a person who helped you during that time? Pray in gratitude for that person today.

✝ Send a card or note to someone who has lost a loved one during this past year.

✝ Spend time prayerfully reviewing your Lenten Plan (page 8), making any adjustments that you think are needed.

 ## Closing Prayer

Pray together:

*Lord Jesus, when I experience wilderness times, let me never forget God's unqualified mercy.*
*As I face times of testing, give me the grace to choose life.*
*Guide me through this Lenten season with a*
*renewed desire to entrust my life into your hands. Amen.*

## Looking Ahead

To prepare for the next session, read the following:

• Second Sunday of Lent: Transformed in the Light

• Matthew 17:1-9

## Monday

 **Pray**

*"Let the words of my mouth and the thought of my heart find favor before you, O Lord, my rock and my redeemer."* (Psalm 19:15)

 **Read** *Matthew 25:31–46*

**Summary:** *"Amen I say to you, what you did not do for one of these least ones, you did not do for me."* (Matthew 25:45)

*Spend two minutes in silence. Then repeat this passage from Scripture and let it speak to your heart.*

 **Meditate**

What might we do this Lent to become the community of Matthew 25, a community that cares for the needs of people? Maybe instead of passing up rocky road ice cream, we will pass on the love of Christ by feeding our neighbors; instead of refraining from buying a piece of clothing during Lent, we will buy a set of new clothing for a person in need; or instead of giving up logging on to Facebook, we will log on to the website of a worthy cause and make a donation. Be creative in your Lenten disciplines, asking always what more you can do for those in need.

# Live Lent!

I will reflect on the concrete actions of love and mercy described in this scene from the Gospel and do one thing today to help a person in need.

 **Pray**

*Lord Jesus, give me the grace to have self-giving care for all my sisters and brothers, especially those in most need. Amen.*

**Pray**

*"Glorify the Lord with me; let us together extol his name. I sought the Lord, and he answered me and delivered me from all my fears."* (Psalm 34: 4-5)

 **Read** Matthew 6:7-15

**Summary:** *"Jesus said to his disciples: 'In praying, do not babble like the pagans, who think that they will be heard because of their many words. Do not be like them. Your Father knows what you need before you ask him.'"* (Matthew 6: 7-8)

*Spend two minutes in silence. Then repeat this passage from Scripture and let it speak to your heart.*

 **Meditate**

The heart of the Lord's Prayer, the model for all our prayer, is a resolve to commit our own will and action to fulfilling the will of God. Prayer isn't about manipulating God to do what we want; it's about humbly entrusting our troubles to a God who listens to our prayer and whose will is that we flourish as human beings.

# Live Lent!

I will write down all my concerns and persons I am worrying about and entrust them to God.

 **Pray**

*Loving God, I entrust this day to you. Give me a heart, simple and sincere, that is filled with a deep love for you and your will. Amen.*

**Pray**

*"A clean heart create for me, O God, and a steadfast spirit renew within me."* (Psalm 51:12)

 **Read** *Luke 11:29-32*

**Summary:**  *"While still more people gathered in the crowd, Jesus said to them, 'This generation is an evil generation; it seeks a sign, but no sign will be given it, except the sign of Jonah. Just as Jonah became a sign to the Ninevites, so will the Son of Man be to this generation.'"* (Luke 11: 29-30)

*Spend two minutes in silence. Then repeat this passage from Scripture and let it speak to your heart.*

 **Meditate**

Lent is an opportunity for us to hear again Jesus' call to change our hearts and live according to the Gospel. Will we be like the crowd and ask for another sign, or will we follow the path of the Ninevites and repent of our selfish ways and follow Christ? No half-hearted response to God's unconditional love revealed in Jesus is sufficient.

## Live Lent!

I will reflect on and name the signs of God's love and compassion in my life and commit my life today to hearing and following Christ's Word.

 **Pray**

*Good and gracious God, open my eyes to the signs of your love today. Cleanse my heart, open my ears to your voice, and renew my spirit. Amen.*

**Pray**

*"Lord, on the day I called for help, you answered me."* (Psalm 138: 3)

 **Read** *Matthew 7:7-12*

**Summary:** "Ask and it will be given you; seek and you will find; knock and the door will be opened to you. For everyone who asks, receives; and the one who seeks, finds; and to the one who knocks, the door will be opened."

(Matthew 7:7-8)

*Spend two minutes in silence. Then repeat this passage from Scripture and let it speak to your heart.*

 **Meditate**

In this section of the Sermon on the Mount, Jesus concludes his instruction on how the disciples are to live, encouraging them to pray—to ask, to seek, and to knock. Knocking on the doors of mercy is a Jewish expression of prayer. Prayer opens the doors of mercy, and God acts. So, then, prayer is more about divine goodness than about human persistence; it is about relationship with God.

## Live Lent!

I will knock on the door of mercy and ask God to help a person who is most in need of God's healing embrace.

 **Pray**

*Loving God, thank you for inviting me into a relationship with you and for answering my prayer with gracious and wise gifts. Bless me with a portion of your generous spirit, so I may freely give to others wherever I find an open door. Amen.*

**Pray**

*"Out of the depths I call to you, O Lord; Lord, hear my voice! Let your ears be attentive to my voice in supplication.*

*If you, O Lord, mark iniquities, Lord, who can stand? But with you is forgiveness so that you may be revered."* (Psalm 130: 1-4)

 **Read** *Matthew 5:20-26*

**Summary:** "Therefore, if you bring your gift to the altar, and there recall that your brother has anything against you, leave your gift there at the altar, go first and be reconciled with your brother, and then come and offer your gift." *(Matthew 5:23-24)*

*Spend two minutes in silence. Then repeat this passage from Scripture and let it speak to your heart.*

 **Meditate**

In this gospel passage, Jesus teaches his followers that they are to consider reconciliation and forgiveness even more important than worship at the altar. The God who is filled with compassion and forgiveness pours mercy upon us, inviting us, through God's grace, to do the same. Don't waste your life in bitterness; move forward in the freedom of God—practice forgiveness.

# Live Lent!

I will place myself in the presence of the Lord and ask if there someone in my life that I haven't been able to forgive. I will write that person's name on a piece of paper, keep it in the place where I pray, and ask God to show me a path to reconciliation.

**Pray**

*God of mercy and compassion, soften my heart toward those
who have hurt me. Give me the grace to practice the habit of
forgiveness. Help me be like Jesus, the compassion of God. Amen.*

## Saturday

 **Pray**

*"Blessed are they whose way is blameless, who walk in the law of
the Lord.*

*Blessed are they who observe his decrees, who seek God with all
their heart." (Psalm 119:1-2)*

 **Read** *Matthew 5:43-48*

**Summary:**   *For if you love those who love you, what recompense
will you have? Do not the tax collectors do the same?
And if you greet your brothers and sisters only, what
is unusual about that? Do not the pagans do the
same? So be perfect, just as your heavenly Father is
perfect." (Matthew 5:46-48)*

*Spend two minutes in silence. Then repeat this passage from Scripture and
let it speak to your heart.*

 **Meditate**

Many of us have trouble with the word "perfection." How can we be
perfect? Jesus does not call us to moral perfection—an impossible
ideal for us to obtain—or to perfection in the legalistic sense of
keeping all the religious laws. The biblical word for perfection used in
this gospel passage means "wholeness." So, then, the perfection Jesus
exhorts us to is to serve God wholeheartedly, to be single-minded in
our devotion to God and in our striving to love our neighbor—not

only our closest circle of friends and family but also the stranger, and especially people who are most in need.

## Live Lent!

I will be wholehearted today as Jesus asks of me and reach out in charity to someone who is outside my circle of family and friends.

 **Pray**

*Lord Jesus, I place my weak and imperfect self before you and give you my life this day. Help me to live a life of charity and sacrifice in search of perfection, seeking and serving you in the midst of my struggles, doubts, and fears. Amen.*

*Transformed in the Light*

## Suggested Environment

A small table with a burning candle and a Bible opened to the gospel reading for this session. Consider decorating the table with violet, the liturgical color of the Lenten season. Drape a small section of white cloth, such as a scarf or handkerchief, alongside the Bible.

### Liturgical Readings for the
### Second Sunday of Lent

GENESIS 12: 1-4a
*God's Promise to Abram*

PSALM 33:4-5, 18-19, 20, 22
*We place our trust in God.*

2 TIMOTHY 1:8b-10
*Salvation comes through grace.*

MATTHEW 17:1-9 (25)
*Jesus is transfigured before them.*

## Focus

God calls us to listen to and believe in his Son.

**Opening Song** (To download, visit ocp.org/renew-music.)

"*Transfigure Us, O Lord,*" Bob Hurd, or "*Change Our Hearts,*" Rory Cooney

 **Opening Prayer**

Form two groups and pray alternately from Psalm 33, with everyone repeating the response.

**R. Lord, let your mercy be on us, as we place our trust in you.**

**Side 1:**    *Upright is the word of the Lord,*
*and all his works are trustworthy.*
*He loves justice and right;*
*of the kindness of the Lord the earth is full.*

**R. Lord, let your mercy be on us, as we place our trust in you.**

**Side 2:**    *See, the eyes of the Lord*
*are upon those who fear him,*
*upon those who hope for his kindness,*
*To deliver them from death*
*and preserve them in spite of famine.*

**R. Lord, let your mercy be on us, as we place our trust in you.**

**All:**    *Our soul waits for the Lord,*
*who is our help and our shield.*
*May your kindness, O Lord, be upon us*
*who have put our hope in you.*

**R. Lord, let your mercy be on us, as we place our trust in you.**

 **The Gospel of the Lord**

*"From the shining cloud the Father's voice is heard: 'This is my beloved Son, hear him.'"* (Matthew 17:5)

**Read aloud** *Matthew 17:1-9*

## Reflect

*What word, phrase, or image from the scripture reading touches your heart or connects to your experience? Share with the group, or write your response here:*

_____

_____

_____

_____

## Old Testament Connections

The language of this gospel passage is suffused with references to the Old Testament, suggesting that this narrative is expressed in theological terms. There is first of all the holy mountain where the presence of the Lord God is most dramatically apparent, as in the stories of Moses (Ex 24:12-18) and Elijah (1 Kgs 19:8-18). The Lord dwells "on high."

Here Jesus is radiant, and our thoughts flash back to the glorious angel in the Book of Daniel (10:5-6). The garments of Jesus are pure white, as in Daniel 7:9 where the "Ancient One" is depicted in garments that are white as snow. The book of Revelation uses the same imagery to describe those who are saved, all adorned in white (Rev 4:4 and 7: 9, 13-14).

Peter blurts out, "I will make three tents here, one for you, one for Moses, and one for Elijah" and we think of the Jewish Feast of Tabernacles in the time of Jesus, a joyous gathering, a time for enjoying the fruits of the harvest and sleeping in make-shift shelters.

Moses and Elijah are the great prophets—Moses the teacher, Elijah the doer. But Jesus between them, at the center, joining in his ministry the prophetic missions of each. He stands at the center, between the prophets of old.

Out of the cloud comes the voice of God. The cloud that guided the Israelites in the wilderness made visible the divine presence among them. It led them to the Promised Land. In the Gospel, the voice that sounds from the cloud guides us to listen to Jesus. He is the prophet of the future predicted by Moses, as we read in the Book of Deuteronomy (18:15). God has just now identified that long-awaited prophet!

And the disciples begin to understand the message of this mysterious person: It is about the resurrection that follows the passion. It addresses, but does not fully answer, one of the deepest mysteries of human life: Why suffering? Yet suffering, endured as Jesus endured it, ultimately ends, and one will, indeed, see the face of God and live.

*Adapted from a reflection by Martin Lang in* Matthew: Come, Follow Me, *part of the* RENEW Scripture Series.

## Reflect

*In the mysterious event known as the Transfiguration, the voice of the Creator tells us to listen to our Savior. In what ways do you listen to Jesus? What do you hear? Share with the group, and/or write your response here.*

_____

_____

_____

_____

 **Meditation**

Fifteen years before my Dad's death, he had a powerful transfiguration experience, and it carried him through the suffering of the last months of his life. My parents traveled with a group to Mexico, and they visited the shrine of Our Lady of Guadalupe. My father, who was a retired New York City policeman, a faithful Catholic but saltier more than pious, climbed the steps and entered the basilica.

As he told the story, he left my mom and her "cronies" outside the church "gabbing." Standing in the back of the church, he listened to Mass being celebrated in multiple languages. As the priest raised the host, my father experienced the overwhelming presence of God; he described a moment when all the people seemed to be holding hands as if they were one, and light was emanating from the multi-ethnic congregation. He felt paralyzed. As he glanced at the woman next to him there were tears running down her face.

When my parents returned from Mexico my father shared his mountaintop experience with many people, but in the intervening years the story became a distant memory. However, during the last three months of his life, 92 years old and dying from cancer, he recalled this mysterious event. The memory of his mountaintop experience strengthened him as he endured his cross. My father, changed by his God experience at Guadalupe and strengthened by the memory of Christ's light, was borne through his dark time and peacefully into the hands of a loving God.

I wonder if one of the reasons God gave the disciples the transfiguration experience was to carry them through the dark times to come. We, too, will be transformed when we share in the resurrection of Jesus. But that glory is already within us. For it does not come from the outside but from the inside. The glory of the Lord inside my dad gave him the strength to move with confidence from the cross to the resurrection.

## Reflect

*How does your faith help you to bear the crosses that come your way?*

_____

_____

_____

_____

*What change can you bring about in your life this Lent that will reveal Christ to others through you?*

_____

_____

_____

_____

*Jesus did not want Peter, James, and John to be preoccupied with a vision of glory before they had grasped the meaning of his death and resurrection and applied it to their life and work in the here and now.*

*In what ways have you experienced or witnessed new life following a death?*

_____

_____

_____

_____

# Live Lent!

† Recall a time when you experienced God's transforming presence in your life. Write about it, or share your story with someone.

† Lent is a time for many people to commit to finding more time in their lives for prayer. Try once a day to stop what you're doing, close your eyes, and thank God for something in your day for which you are grateful.

† Spend time prayerfully reviewing your Lenten Plan (page 8), making any adjustments that you think are needed.

 **Closing Prayer**

Pray together:

*Lord, you are with us on the mountaintops of life.*
*In those moments, we glimpse the grandeur*
*of your presence and the splendor of your promise.*
*Let us hold these experiences in our hearts*
*even as we return to our everyday lives.*
*Let our sight be pure and our hearts filled with hope*
*this Lenten season as we await the promised glory of your*
*resurrection. Amen.*

## Looking Ahead

To prepare for the next session, read the following:

• John 4:5-42

• Session Three: In Christ, our thirst is quenched

## Monday

 **Pray**

*"Remember not against us the iniquities of the past; may your compassion quickly come to us, for we are brought very low."*
*(Psalm 79:8)*

 **Read** Luke 6:36-38

**Summary:** *"Jesus said to his disciples: 'Be merciful, just as your Father is merciful. Stop judging and you will not be judged. Stop condemning and you will not be condemned. Forgive and you will be forgiven.'" (Luke 6:33-27)*

*Spend two minutes in silence. Then repeat this passage from Scripture and let it speak to your heart.*

 **Meditation**

If we are honest, we know we judge others a lot, often with little evidence and even less compassion. We lack compassion for the weaknesses of others and ourselves. Our media outlets, too, are quick to condemn and slow to retract. I always try to remind myself to not judge people's motives even if their actions appear to be wrong. Jesus reminds us in today's gospel reading that the way of God is one of mercy and forgiveness. The more compassion we have for others; the more compassion we will receive.

# Live Lent!

I will be mindful today of how quickly I judge others, in the media, in my interactions, and especially in my conversations. I will pray for a generous and more compassionate heart.

---

**Pray**

God of mercy and forgiveness, free me from my small judgmental ways and expand my heart to reach out to others in love. Amen.

## Tuesday

 **Pray**

"Wash yourselves clean! Put away your misdeeds from before my eyes; cease doing evil; learn to do good. Make justice your aim: redress the wronged, hear the orphan's plea, defend the widow." (Isaiah 1:16-17)

 **Read** Matthew 23:1-12

**Summary:**    "Therefore, do and observe all things whatsoever they tell you, but do not follow their example. For they preach but they do not practice. They tie up heavy burdens hard to carry and lay them on people's shoulders, but they will not lift a finger to move them. All their works are performed to be seen." (Matthew 23:3-5a)

*Spend two minutes in silence. Then repeat this passage from Scripture and let it speak to your heart.*

 **Meditation**

I think there is an important reminder for us in these words of Jesus from today's gospel reading: our actions are to be consistent with our words. We go to Mass on Sunday, but is our conduct the other six days of the week consistent with what we pray and profess on Sunday? Each one of the prayers at the conclusion of Mass begins with "Go." We are called to move from the Liturgy of the Word and Eucharist to the liturgy of the world. The object of our Christian faith is not to console us and make us feel good, but to exhort us to radically live the Gospel—proclaiming the kingdom of God first by our lives and then by our words.

# Live Lent!

I will think about this past Sunday or the last time I went to Mass. Did I notice the words of the dismissal at the end? I will try to be more faithful to the gospel in all I do today.

 **Pray**

*Good and gracious God, give me the strength to live in accordance with what I profess; give me grace to bear faithful witness, in word and in deed, to your glory and your grace. Help me to honor you with my lips, my heart, and my life. Amen.*

## Wednesday

 **Pray**

*"But my trust is in you, O Lord; I say, 'You are my God.' In your hands is my destiny"* (Psalm 31: 15-16a)

 **Read** *Matthew 20:17-28*

**Summary:** *"But Jesus summoned them and said, 'You know that the rulers of the Gentiles lord it over them, and the great ones make their authority over them felt. But it shall not be so among you. Rather, whoever wishes to be great among you shall be your servant; whoever wishes to be first among you shall be your slave. Just so, the Son of Man did not come to be served but to serve and to give his life as a ransom for many.'"* (Matthew 20:25-28)

*Spend two minutes in silence. Then repeat this passage from Scripture and let it speak to your heart.*

**Meditation**

Jesus' vision of leadership is servanthood, and it corresponds to his alternative vision of kingship. Jesus does not use exalted and powerful terms to describe Christian leaders; instead he uses the word diakonos ("deacon"), which literally means "table servant." All followers of Jesus are called to Christian service wherever we find ourselves. If you will remind yourself at the start of each day that you are God's servant, interruptions won't frustrate you as much, because your agenda will be whatever God wants to bring into your life. Remember, all your time— every moment—belongs to God.

# Live Lent!

I will keep in mind that my time belongs to God. I will reach out in service to someone beyond where my obligation lies. I will not expect anything in return.

 **Pray**

*Jesus, you teach me by your word and life to be a servant of God. Help me see that greatness comes by humble service. Expand my heart and give me a servant's temperament—one that desires to serve others, expecting nothing in return. Amen.*

## Thursday

 **Pray**

*"Blessed are they who hope in the Lord. He is like a tree planted near running water, That yields its fruit in due season, and whose leaves never fade. Whatever he does, prospers." (Psalm 40:5a; Psalm 1:3)*

 **Read** *Luke 16:19-31*

**Summary:** *"Jesus said to the Pharisees: 'There was a rich man*

*who dressed in purple garments and fine linen and dined sumptuously each day. And lying at his door was a poor man named Lazarus, covered with sores, who would gladly have eaten his fill of the scraps that fell from the rich man's table. Dogs even used to come and lick his sores. When the poor man died, he was carried away by angels to the bosom of Abraham. The rich man also died and was buried, and from the netherworld, where he was in torment, he raised his eyes and saw Abraham far off and Lazarus at his side.'"* (Luke 16:19-23)

*Spend two minutes in silence. Then repeat this passage from Scripture and let it speak to your heart.*

 **Meditation**

The parable clearly urges us to share food with those who are hungry, but even deeper than that, it insists we be good neighbors, especially to those most in need. True charity is more than giving a few coins to someone begging on a street corner, or writing a check to the local shelter at Christmas time. It is noticing, caring, and acting on the needs of our sister or brother—it is cultivating an attitude of the heart that suffers with our neighbor and compels us to respond compassionately.

## Live Lent!

I will serve at a local care center before Lent ends. Or, I will search my memory for any times I encountered someone in need and did not help, and I will seek forgiveness.

 **Pray**

*God of compassion, give me a heart of mercy and care and a spirit of committed love. Graciously answer my prayer through Jesus, my brother and companion to anyone in need. Amen.*

**Pray**

*"God so loved the world that he gave his only-begotten Son; so that everyone who believes in him might have eternal life."* (John 3:16)

 **Read** *Matthew 21:33-43, 45, 46*

**Summary:**  *"Jesus said to them, 'Did you never read in the Scriptures: 'The stone that the builders rejected has become the cornerstone; by the Lord has this been done, and it is wonderful in our eyes'?"* (Matthew 21:42)

*Spend two minutes in silence. Then repeat this passage from Scripture and let it speak to your heart.*

 **Meditation**

Quoting from the Hebrew Scriptures, Jesus says, "The stone that the builder rejected has become the cornerstone." Jesus the Christ is the new cornerstone promised by God from the beginning of time to found a new community. But he has been rejected. Christ is the cornerstone upon which you want to build your life; he is your rock and refuge, and he calls you to align your values and beliefs with his will and way. Is Christ the foundation that holds up every facet of your life?

# Live Lent!

I will begin to practice a nightly examination of conscience. First, I will review my day, thinking about how God has blessed me. I will give thanks. Then, I will examine ways in which I have neglected to keep Christ as the cornerstone of my life. I will ask for forgiveness.

 **Pray**

*Loving God, thank you for sending your Son Jesus to be the cornerstone of my life. Give me the grace to build my life on the sure foundation of his teachings. Amen.*

**Pray**

"He pardons all your iniquities, he heals all your ills. He redeems your life from destruction, he crowns you with kindness and compassion." (Psalm 103:3-4)

 **Read** *Luke 15:1-3, 11-32*

**Summary:**  "While he was still a long way off, his father caught sight of him, and was filled with compassion. He ran to his son, embraced him and kissed him. His son said to him, 'Father, I have sinned against heaven and against you; I no longer deserve to be called your son.' But his father ordered his servants, 'Quickly, bring the finest robe and put it on him; put a ring on his finger and sandals on his feet. Take the fattened calf and slaughter it. Then let us celebrate with a feast, because this son of mine was dead, and has come to life again; he was lost, and has been found.' Then the celebration began." (Luke 15:20b-24)

*Spend two minutes in silence. Then repeat this passage from Scripture and let it speak to your heart.*

 **Meditation**

Imagine God waiting with arms outstretched and running to meet you, inviting and cajoling you to turn away from your sinful ways, to let go of your unforgiving heart and commit to a deeper gospel love and living. How will you respond?

## Live Lent!

I will ask the "waiting Father" for the courage to initiate reconciliation with someone I have struggled to forgive. I will first forgive, which is an act of the will, and then discern if God is calling me to take a step toward healing the damaged relationship.

 **Pray**

*Waiting Father, I thank you for your extravagant and reckless love for me. I open my heart and hands to your mercy. Amen.*

# Third Sunday of Lent

*In Christ, our thirst is quenched.*

## Suggested Environment

A small table with a burning candle and a Bible opened to the gospel reading for this session. Consider decorating the table with violet, the liturgical color of the Lenten season. Place a small decorative bowl of water on the table.

### Liturgical Readings for the Third Sunday of Lent

EXODUS 17:3-7
*The Israelites grumble against Moses.*

PSALM 95:1-2, 6-7, 8-9
*Do not harden your heart.*

ROMANS 5:1-2, 5-8
*"Hope does not disappoint, because the love of God has been poured into our hearts."*

JOHN 4:5-42
*Jesus meets the Samaritan woman at the well .*

## Focus

Jesus is the source of new life for the Samaritan woman and for each of us.

**Opening Song** (To download, visit ocp.org/renew-music.)
*"You Are Near,"* or *"River of Glory,"* Daniel L. Schutte

 **Opening Prayer**

Form two groups, and pray alternately from Psalm 95, with everyone repeating the response:

**R. *If today you hear his voice, harden not your hearts.***

**Side 1:**      *Come, let us sing joyfully to the Lord;*
                 *let us acclaim the Rock of our salvation.*
                 *Let us come into his presence with thanksgiving;*
                 *let us joyfully sing psalms to him.*

**R. *If today you hear his voice, harden not your hearts.***

**Side 2:**      *Come, let us bow down in worship;*
                 *let us kneel before the Lord who made us.*
                 *For he is our God,*
                 *and we are the people he shepherds, the flock he*
                 *guides.*

**R. *If today you hear his voice, harden not your hearts.***

**All:**         *Oh, that today you would hear his voice:*
                 *"Harden not your hearts as at Meribah,*
                 *as in the day of Massah in the desert,*
                 *Where your fathers tempted me;*
                 *they tested me though they had seen my works."*

**R. *If today you hear his voice, harden not your hearts.***

 **The Gospel of the Lord**

"Sir, give me this water, so that I may not be thirsty." (John 4:15)

**Read aloud** *John 4:5-42*

## Reflect

*What word, phrase, or image from the scripture reading touches your heart or connects to your experience? Share with the group, or write your response here:*

_____

_____

_____

_____

## Old Testament Connections

The setting for this scene is Samaria, a place to stop for Jesus on the way to Galilee. Samaria is known in the Old Testament for suffering defeat at the hands of the idolatrous and vicious Assyrians, an event historians place around 720 B.C. (2 Kg 17:24-34).

The king of Assyria replaced the people of Samaria with settlers from his own lands. People from five cultural groups were imported, and they came with their false gods. The writer of the passage in the Book of Kings explains that those immigrants brought pagan worship to Samaria and, even though the Assyrian king sent a Levite priest to instruct them in the faith of Israel, they clung to their pagan ways even up to the time the Bible passage was written. That signals for all later readers of the Book of Kings that Samaritans had for many centuries been tinged with the stigma of idolatry. It also enlightens us about the evangelist Luke's story of the Good Samaritan, a "foreigner" who by his charity outstrips the virtue of the Jerusalem priest and Levite, neither of whom stopped to heal the wounds of the suffering traveler (Lk 10:30-37).

In our passage, Jesus instructs a Samaritan woman at a well thought to have been dug by the patriarch Jacob himself, long before the Assyrians came. The water of the ancient well, static and imperfect, is replaced by living water that we now have learned is the life of the Spirit.

There is an interpretation in some biblical circles that sees the five husbands as the false gods brought into Samaria by the five groups. The woman represents the typical Samaritan who needs to be freed from the trappings of lingering paganism. The idea has some credibility, because the pagan gods were called Baals (usually fertility gods). But the word "Baal" in the Bible is often used to mean "a lord," but then again (and this is what convinces some) it is used to designate "a husband."

Why are we told of this story in Samaria?  Perhaps because the Samaritans were one of the first communities to believe in Jesus, evangelized by the apostle Philip, and given the Holy Spirit in the laying on of hands by the apostles Peter and John (Acts 8:4-25).

*Adapted from a reflection by Martin Lang in* John: I Am the Vine, *a forthcoming part of the* RENEW Scripture Series.

## Reflect

*Martin Lang offers a different interpretation for the "five husbands" passage in this story than is typically offered. What was your reaction to that interpretation? In what ways does this perspective alter your own perspective on the woman and her story?*

*Share with the group, and/or write your response here.*

_____

_____

_____

_____

 **Meditation**

Michael and his wife, Rose, were both university professors, accomplished scholars, artists, and delightful characters. When they met, both were divorced and neither Rose, a Catholic, nor Michael, a Jew, practiced a faith. After they were married, Rose, through a priest chaplain at their university, recommitted to her faith, and their marriage was blessed in the Church. Michael began accompanying Rose to Mass.

Michael and Rose selected St. James Cathedral Parish in Brooklyn because of the beautiful liturgies, outstanding adult faith programs, and good preaching. Michael first attended Mass at the Cathedral on Easter Sunday primarily for Rose. He described himself as a "fledging Christian though still primarily a cynic and a doubter." "Coming to St. James was for me then," he wrote, "a decision that I made in renewed agony each Sunday." However, as he listened to the well-prepared homilies and prayed with the community, some of his self-described cynicism began to erode. He continued to search, question, and analyze every aspect of Christianity.

Then, Michael had a "St. Paul experience." While walking across the Brooklyn Bridge on his regular route to work, he suddenly was caught up in the beautiful skyline and had an encounter with Christ—one that shook him to his core. In describing that encounter, he said it was as if "the scales fell from my eyes and my thirst to know Christ became insatiable." He was a medievalist and voraciously read the works of Augustine and Ambrose with a new understanding. He entered the process of the Rite of Christian Initiation of Adults (RCIA) and began his journey toward baptism and incorporation into a life of discipleship. He was baptized at the following Easter Vigil and shared how he was able by God's grace to proclaim in pure faith "I do" to each of his baptismal vows. Michael received the living water of Christ's love, left his old life behind, and continued throughout the rest of his life witnessing to Christ through charitable works and acts of justice. He joined his wife each week in serving meals to the homeless at the Catholic Worker house in New York City.

The story of the woman at the well is a metaphor for Michael's journey to discipleship and a job description for every disciple. In this story, those preparing for baptism recognize themselves as the woman who, by listening to Jesus' word, grows gradually in her understanding of who she is encountering. She leaves behind her water jug of cynicism and emptiness. The Church as well recognizes its mission realized through the woman, who by her witness brings a town of people to encounter for themselves Jesus the Christ, the long-awaited Messiah.

Both Michael and the woman of Samaria encountered Christ in the midst of their everyday routines and, through honest seeking and bold questioning, grew in their relationship with him.

Many of us were baptized as infants and simply inherited our faith. But there is a point when, as adults, we need to reexamine and recommit ourselves to our baptismal promises—to say yes to Christ and to a live as his disciples. Even if we have made an adult commitment to Christ, we sometimes lose our way and find ourselves thirsty, disoriented, and unsatisfied, and we drift toward wells of superficial pleasures, quick fixes, and strange gods. This week we are called to come to the well of life-giving water, spend time with Jesus, bring our questions, burdens, and sinfulness and ask Christ to draw us ever closer to our merciful God.

## Reflect

*The author of this Gospel emphasizes the fact that the Samaritan woman encountered Jesus while she was going about a routine chore. How have you encountered Jesus while you were taking care of business seemingly far removed from your personal life?*

_____

_____

_____

_____

*The woman at the well speaks frankly to Jesus. How do you speak to him? What words do you use? What is it like to be completely candid with the Savior?*

_____

_____

_____

_____

*The Samaritan woman is so inspired by Jesus that she must run and share the experience with her community. When has an encounter with Jesus made you want to spread his gospel? Is there someone in your life with whom you might share your faith through words or charitable works during this Lent?*

_____

_____

_____

# Live Lent!

- † One action Michael took to live his faith was to serve meals each week at a soup kitchen. What action may you take in your community as you recommit yourself to be Christ's disciple?

- † Catholic Relief Services supports global water initiatives that help bring clean water and proper sanitation to areas in need. Consider donating to this program. You can find out what they do and how to contribute at crs.org/wash.

- † Spend time prayerfully reviewing your Lenten Plan (page 8), making any adjustments that you think may be needed.

 ## Closing Prayer

Pray together:

*Lord Jesus, you stopped at the well because you were thirsty and yet we were the ones who were refreshed. You are the living water who brings us new life. Pour your grace into us, and let it overflow from our cup to others who need to be restored in your love. Amen.*

## Looking Ahead

To prepare for the next session, read the following:

- Fourth Sunday of Lent: Jesus heals those who are blind.
- John 9:1-41.

## Monday

### Pray

As the deer longs for the running waters, so my soul longs for you, O God. (Psalm 42:2)

### Read Luke 4: 24-30

**Summary:**   "Jesus said to the people in the synagogue at Nazareth: 'Amen I say to you. . . . It was to none of these that Elijah was sent, but only to a widow in Zarephath in the land of Sidon. Again there were many lepers in Israel since the time of Elisha the prophet; yet not one of them was cleansed, but only Naaman the Syrian.' When the people in the synagogue heard this, they were all filled with fury. They rose up and drove Jesus out of town. . . ." (Luke 4:24,26-28)

*Spend two minutes in silence. Then repeat this passage from Scripture and let it speak to your heart.*

### Meditation

There was an article in the *Columbus Dispatch* about Jim Rush's garden. Usually, backyard gardens are extensions of people's homes and are only for a small circle of neighbors and family. The opposite is true of Jim's garden. The sign in his front yard sums up his philosophy: "Garden is Open. Please Stop In—All Are Welcome," and people do stop in. Jim believes a garden is to be shared.

Jim's open and inclusive garden is like the kingdom of God preached by Jesus—all are welcome. Jesus is in his own town, preaching and healing. At first, his neighbors are delighted to have a prophet in their midst. They consider it a great blessing until it becomes clear that Jesus is reading the Scriptures differently. The hometown crowd interprets the Scriptures to mean that God's kingdom is open exclusively to them. Jesus' philosophy is opposite—all are welcome to receive God's gracious love and blessings. Jesus leaves no one out. He connects his ministry to the prophets Elijah and Elisha; like them, he opens his ministry of deliverance and healing to those beyond the Jewish community. In fact, he welcomes the whole world in.

This gospel scene reminds us that God's grace cannot be fenced in like a private garden. It is not limited to the boundaries of any town, nation, church, group, gender, or race. The garden of God's love and healing power is open to all who enter in faith.

# Live Lent!

I will examine the past week and ask if I have excluded someone unnecessarily, neglected to welcome another into conversation, or in other ways have been inhospitable. I will consider how to change my attitude and learn to be more open.

 **Pray**

*Generous God, help me to expand my notion of community and welcome all kinds of people into my heart and life. Give me the grace to transcend the boundaries of community and the limits on love that I sometimes build. Amen.*

## Tuesday

 **Pray**

*"Your ways, O Lord, make known to me; teach me your paths, Guide me in your truth and teach me, for you are God my savior."* (Psalm 25:4-5a)

 **Read** *Matthew 18:21-35*

**Summary:**    *"Peter approached Jesus and asked him, 'Lord, if my brother sins against me, how often must I forgive*

*him? As many as seven times?' Jesus answered, 'I say to you, not seven times but seventy-seven times.'"*
(Matthew 18:21-22)

*Spend two minutes in silence. Then repeat this passage from Scripture and let it speak to your heart.*

 **Meditation**

On October 5, 2006, a troubled man barricaded himself in an Amish schoolhouse in the rural town of Nickel Mines, Pennsylvania. He dismissed the boys and shot ten of the girls—five were killed. Less than forty-eight hours later, the grandfather of one of the slain girls was standing next to his granddaughter's body as it was being prepared for burial. He said to a group of boys gathered around, "We must not think evil of this man." He went on to urge them to forgive the killer, who had taken his own life. The community itself embraced the widow of the killer, inviting her to the funerals, telling her that she would be welcome to stay in their community. As cash donations from across the country began to pour in for the families of the victims, they insisted on sharing the money with her. This story of the Amish response to such a heinous act is a sign of God's amazing grace at work within a community: healing broken relationships, effecting harmony, creating peace, and restoring wholeness.

Peter's proposal to forgive seven times sounds incredibly generous. However, Jesus' response to Peter's proposal goes far beyond solely increasing the number of times to forgive. Jesus' pronouncement is about the nature of forgiveness—deep and radical gospel living.

# Live Lent!

I will write down the name of someone I have struggled to forgive, place the slip of paper in my hand, and pray the Lord's Prayer. I will work all day at forgiving, letting go, and discerning if I am called, with the help of God, to take steps to mend the relationship.

**Pray**

Merciful God, forgive me my trespasses and help me forgive those who have harmed me. I ask this through the merciful and compassionate heart of Christ. Amen.

## Wednesday

 **Pray**

"Your words, Lord, are Spirit and life; you have the words of everlasting life." *(John 6:63c, 68c)*

 **Read** *Matthew 5:17-19*

**Summary:**     "'But whoever obeys and teaches these commandments will be called greatest in the Kingdom of heaven.'" *(Matthew 5:19)*

*Spend two minutes in silence. Then repeat this passage from Scripture and let it speak to your heart.*

 **Meditation**

Jesus was a faithful Jew and affirmed the fundamental goodness of the Law and the prophets—the core of the Hebrew Bible. He reminded the disciples that he did not come to replace the Law but to fulfill it. However, this fulfillment does not always mean a mere continuation of the original law; it also means moving beyond it or more deeply into it. Later in Matthew's Gospel, Jesus proclaimed that mercy, justice, love, and covenant fidelity were the weightier matters of the Law by which the rest was to be judged. For Jesus, obeying the Law was not to agonize over every detail and scrupulously follow it but to live its spirit—radically giving over oneself to love of God and neighbor.

# Live Lent!

I will pray today for humility, and say a kind word to a stranger today.

**Pray**

*Loving God, help us to obey your law in the spirit of mercy, justice, and love. Infuse in me a new spirit as I struggle this day to choose love in my innermost thoughts and my actions. Jesus, have mercy on me. Amen.*

## Thursday

 **Pray**

*"Oh, that today you would hear his voice: 'Harden not your hearts....'"* (Psalm 95:7b-8a)

 **Read** *Luke 11:14-23*

**Summary:**   *"He (Jesus) was driving out a demon that was mute, and when the demon had gone out, the mute person spoke and the crowds were amazed. Some of them said, 'By the power of Beelzebul, the prince of demons, he drives out demons....' But he knew their thoughts and said to them... 'But if it is by the finger of God that I drive out demons, then the Kingdom of God has come upon you.'"* (Luke 14-15, 17, 20)

*Spend two minutes in silence. Then repeat this passage from Scripture and let it speak to your heart.*

 **Meditation**

The "finger of God" is a biblical phrase referring to miraculous acts done through God's power. Poetry, art, and film have explored this image, but it is most commonly discovered in ordinary life. We live in a world where God's fingerprints are found in the unlikeliest of places. In today's gospel passage, Jesus drives out the demon from the mute man by the "finger of God." The man's voice is restored. How often do we recognize the finger of God working in and through us? How often do we stop to look?

# Live Lent!

I will watch for the "finger of God" in the ordinary circumstances of my day and offer a prayer of thanks each time I recognize it.

 **Pray**

*God of surprises, help me to recognize your presence and power in my everyday life. Help me comprehend that it is you tapping me on the shoulder and showing me the way. Soften my heart and open my ears so I might receive, listen, and act upon your word this day. Amen.*

## Friday

 **Pray**

*"O that my people would listen to me, that Israel would walk in my ways,...But Israel will feed with the finest wheat, I will satisfy them with honey from the rock...." (Psalm 81:14, 17)*

 **Read** *Mark 12:28-34*

**Summary:**  *"'Which is the first of all the commandments?' Jesus replied, 'The first is this: Hear, O Israel! The Lord our God is Lord alone! You shall love the Lord your God with all your heart, with all your soul, with all your mind, and with all your strength. The second is this: You shall love your neighbor as yourself.'" (Mark 12:28b-31)*

*Spend two minutes in silence. Then repeat this passage from Scripture and let it speak to your heart.*

 **Meditation**

In today's gospel passage, we hear the Great Commandment pressing us to walk on two feet—love of God and love of neighbor. The commitment to help our poorest sisters and brothers is not an option but an expression of our love for God. The conversion that Lent invites us to is not only a turning away from sin and a turning toward God with single-hearted devotion, but also a turning toward our neighbor with a generous heart and empathetic spirit.

# Live Lent!

I will do a random act of kindness today as an expression of my love for God.

 **Pray**

*Loving God, help me to walk as a Christian disciple with a single-hearted love for you and a generous love of my neighbor. I ask this in the name of Jesus, the compassion of God, and through the Holy Spirit, the fountain of love. Amen.*

## Saturday

 **Pray**

*"Have mercy on me, O God, in your goodness; in the greatness of your compassion wipe out my offense. Thoroughly wash me from my guilt; and of my sin cleanse me."* (Psalm 51:3-4)

 **Read** *Luke 18:11-13*

**Summary:**  *"The Pharisee took up his position and spoke this prayer to himself, 'O God, I thank you that I am not like the rest of humanity—greedy, dishonest, adulterous— or even like this tax collector. I fast twice a week, and I pay tithes on my whole income.' But the tax collector stood off at a distance and would not even raise his eyes to heaven but beat his breast and prayed, 'O God, be merciful to me, a sinner.'"* (Luke 18:11-13)

*Spend two minutes in silence. Then repeat this passage from Scripture and let it speak to your heart.*

 **Meditation**

During a football game I was watching, a receiver dropped a would-be touchdown pass. He immediately fell to his knees, lowered his head, and beat his chest three times. This act of humility touched even a hard-nosed fan like me.

In today's gospel parable, Jesus speaks of both the posture and prayer of a Pharisee and of a tax collector. The Pharisee separates himself from others in order to remain pure. He begins his prayer by addressing God and then continues in the first person. His prayer is all about himself and how righteous he is. He is aware of the tax collector in the temple, and he regards him and others like him with contempt. As the Pharisee's prayer continues, he is absorbed and impressed with his own virtue and asks nothing of God. By contrast, the tax collector, who was often guilty of overcharging his neighbors, stands "off at a distance"—thereby acknowledging his unworthiness before God. He beats his breast as a humble sign of remorse and grief. His prayer echoes today's psalm, "Have mercy on me, O God."

This parable is not only about the proper posture for prayer but also speaks of the way the Pharisee regards the tax collector. He totally dismisses him. The Pharisee has lots of religious virtue and piety, but for his neighbor, the tax collector, he has only judgment. Once again, we hear the truth—only those who show mercy and forgiveness to others will receive mercy and forgiveness.

# Live Lent!

I will be mindful of the areas of my life that need God's mercy and forgiveness. With courage and gratitude, I will open my heart and mind to those amazing gifts.

 **Pray**

*Compassionate Father, have mercy on me, a sinner. Bless me with the virtue of humility and give me a heart full of mercy, especially for those I find difficult to love. Amen.*

---

# Fourth Sunday of Lent

*Jesus heals those who are blind.*

## Suggested Environment

A small table with a burning candle and a Bible opened to the gospel reading for this session. Consider decorating the table with violet, the liturgical color of the Lenten season. Place a small lump of clay (made from soil mixed with water) on a plate near the candle.

### Liturgical Readings for the Fourth Sunday of Lent

1 SAMUEL 16:1b, 6-7, 10-13a
*The anointing of David*

PSALM 23:1-3a, 3b-4, 5, 6
*"The Lord is my shepherd, there is nothing I shall want."*

EPHESIANS 5:8-14
*"Live as children of the light."*

JOHN 9:1-41
*The healing of a blind man and the challenge to the Pharisees*

## Focus

If we are receptive, Christ will heal our blindness.

**Opening Song** (To download, visit ocp.org/renew-music.)
*"The Cry of the Poor,"* John Foley, SJ

**Opening Prayer**

Form two groups and pray alternately from Psalm 23, with everyone repeating the response:

**R. *The Lord is my shepherd; there is nothing I shall want.***

**Side 1:**     *The Lord is my shepherd; I shall not want.*
              *In verdant pastures he gives me repose;*
              *beside restful waters he leads me;*
              *he refreshes my soul.*

**R. *The Lord is my shepherd; there is nothing I shall want.***

**Side 2:**     *He guides me in right paths*
              *for his name's sake.*
              *Even though I walk in the dark valley*
              *I fear no evil; for you are at my side*
              *With your rod and your staff*
              *that give me courage.*

**R. *The Lord is my shepherd; there is nothing I shall want.***

**Side 1:**     *You spread the table before me*
              *in the sight of my foes;*
              *you anoint my head with oil;*
              *my cup overflows.*

**R. *The Lord is my shepherd; there is nothing I shall want.***

**Side 2:**     *Only goodness and kindness follow me*
              *all the days of my life;*
              *and I shall dwell in the house of the Lord*
              *for years to come.*

**R. *The Lord is my shepherd; there is nothing I shall want.***

##  The Gospel of the Lord

"I am the light of the world."

*Read aloud* John 9:1-41

## Reflect

*What word, phrase, or image from the scripture reading touches your heart or connects to your experience? Share with the group, or write your response here:*

_____

_____

_____

_____

## Old Testament Connections

The reading (1 Sm 16:1b,6,7,10-13) that the liturgy presents with our gospel passage this Sunday tells about David being chosen by God and anointed by Samuel for David's later role as king and religious leader. God calls through his prophet Samuel, and David responds, and the community of faith is enormously enriched. David's psalms and his efforts to preserve the faith of Israel make him a model for kingship, though he is not without sin. The lesson for our time: faith-filled servants, like Samuel and perhaps we, may become the instruments of grace for others, by our example and our kindness.

The underpinnings of Christian faith lay in the Hebrew Scriptures, and those Scriptures play an immense role in the writing of the Gospel of John as they do in the writing of the others. Isaiah, a prophetic writer favored by evangelists, witnessed most of the influential people of Jerusalem—prophets, magistrates, scholars, and skilled workers—deported to Babylon (modern Iraq).

Isaiah saw this event as a result of Israel's unfaithfulness to God. Yet he was convinced that God would never permit his people to drown in a swirling sea of false gods and false values. In words nearly impossible to believe at the time, he offered hope in a future when God would again rescue his people: "On that day the deaf shall hear the words of a scroll; And out of gloom and darkness, the eyes of the blind shall see" (Is 29:18).

The God of Israel, who loved his people unconditionally, would come to their aid—and he did, just five decades later when Cyrus, the ruler from Persia (modern Iran), released the Israelite deportees and even offered funds for the rebuilding of their Temple in Jerusalem.

Isaiah's texts were used as visions of the future for Jews in the decades following the destruction of Jerusalem, as they sought a reasonable explanation for the catastrophe. Christians, many of them Jews of Greek culture in the time of John's Gospel, saw Jesus as God's liberating promise fulfilled for his people. Now people of all nations could know God's love as taught by Jesus and experience the fulfillment of the divine promise.

If we may borrow from the Gospel of Luke, directed largely to Greeks at the time, we find it offers a powerful scene that clearly demonstrates Jesus as the fulfiller of the prophecies of Isaiah. Jesus rises in the synagogue at Nazareth and reads a passage from Isaiah (61:1-2a):

> "The Spirit of the Lord is upon me,
> because he has anointed me
> to bring glad tidings to the poor
> He has sent me to proclaim liberty to the captives
> and recovery of sight to the blind,
> to let the oppressed go free,
> to proclaim the year acceptable to the Lord." (Lk 4: 18-19)

God's saving plan was being implemented in the here and now, and even Greek converts understood it as applying to their lives. This is also the central message in the healings we see in John's Gospel: the paralyzed man walks; the blind man sees. Jesus is the instrument of God's love in these freeing acts.

It is an astounding message for all of humankind: all are to be free—first free from the bonds of sin, then free from the oppressions that burden our lives. This is magnified in John's Gospel by the blind man being healed on the Sabbath contrary to the teaching of rabbis who have interpreted the command about the Sabbath in a very limiting way. Christian faith is intended to be a freeing, exhilarating experience, and finding the liberating factors in human life, such as looking for cures from disease, creating laws that unburden people, and framing society so that poor people may rise out of poverty, are noble tasks for those who live their faith.

*Adapted from a reflection by Martin Lang in* John: I Am the Vine, *a forthcoming part of the* RENEW *Scripture Series.*

## Reflect

*The God of Israel is often characterized as a God of judgment, an evaluation with which many Jewish and Christian scholars take issue. Do you think of God in terms of judgment or in terms of mercy? Has your view changed over time. Why? Share with the group, or write your response here:*

_____

_____

_____

_____

 **Meditation**

I was living in Elegido, a poor town in the Dominican Republic. We had electricity a few hours each morning and a few hours each night. I entered into the daily ritual of waiting, with the family I was staying with, for the light to come.

Power was restored at a different hour each evening. As the light came to a particular block, the people would break out in cheers. You could hear the light coming before you could see it. I waited with anticipation as the light gradually came to our block, and then I joined in the cheering. Restoring power to the town of Elegido was a process, and it took time before the entire town was basking in light.

The powerful story of the man born blind gradually moving from blindness to sight, and then from sight to insight, reminds me that conversion, too, is a process. Jesus restores the man's physical sight, but that is just the beginning. After Jesus heals him, the Pharisees ask what the man has to say about Jesus. He begins simply by calling Jesus a "man"—a wonderful person who did a great deed for him. Later, when asked again, he calls Jesus a "prophet." Then finally he professes Jesus as the "Son of God."

Jesus, the light of the world, had moved the man from blindness to sight and, more importantly, from sight to insight.

Lent is a good opportunity to take time to reflect on your relationship with God. Are you growing in your intimacy with God? Are you living the Gospel more deeply? If you are not moving forward spiritually, maybe you are stuck and need to find a way to grow.

## Reflect

*The Gospel contrasts darkness with light in both the man's physical blindness and the spiritual blindness of the Pharisees. Where do you see spiritual blindness in your everyday surroundings? What part can you play in dispelling the darkness with the light of Christ?*

_____

_____

_____

_____

*The blind man's perception of Jesus moves from "man" through "prophet" to "Son of God." Has your experience of Jesus changed over time? How do you see Jesus today differently than in earlier chapters of your life? What brought about those changes?*

_____

_____

_____

_____

*Do you have any blind spots to address? What are they, and what can you do to overcome them?*

_____

_____

_____

_____

# Live Lent!

    † Recall a favorite memory of light scattering darkness and hold that image in your mind today as a reminder to thank God for the ability to move from darkness to insight about his presence in your life.

    † Are you aware of someone—perhaps an older person—who is struggling with his or her eyesight? Consider how you can help: by offering to read to that person, by helping that person acquire recorded books, by assisting with household chores that may be daunting for someone with poor vision, by offering to accompany the person on an outing. Or, determine if there is a local organization that helps senior citizens who are losing or have lost their eyesight, and ask if you can volunteer.

    † Spend time prayerfully reviewing your Lenten Plan, (page 8), making any adjustments that you think are needed.

 **Closing Prayer**

Pray together:

_Jesus, Son of Man, your light shines into human life and illuminates the places where we are blind and resistant. Bathe us in the glow of your healing love and free us from the darkness that impedes us from seeing and following you. Amen._

## Looking Ahead

To prepare for the next session, read the following:

- John 11:1-45
- Session Five: Jesus raises his friend, Lazarus, from the dead.

## Monday

 **Pray**

*"'Hear O Lord, and have pity on me; O Lord, be my helper.' You changed my mourning into dancing; O Lord my God, forever will I give you thanks."* (Psalm 30:11-12a, 13b)

 **Read** *John 4:43-54*

**Summary:** "Jesus said to him 'Unless you people see signs and wonders, you will not believe.' The royal official said to him, 'Sir, come down before my child dies.' Jesus said him, 'You may go; your son will live.' The man believed what Jesus said to him and left." (John 4:48-50)

*Spend two minutes in silence. Then repeat this passage from Scripture and let it speak to your heart.*

 **Meditation**

Signs provide an opening to faith, but signs in themselves do not guarantee faith, nor is faith dependent on them. Jesus healed many people and performed powerful works, yet many still did not believe in him. In the incident described in today's gospel reading, Jesus performed another sign, and the royal official not only rejoiced in the miracle of his son's healing but also came to see beyond the miracle itself. When a miracle is fully understood as a sign, it points to who Jesus truly is—the giver of life—and Jesus points to who God is, and this is the basis for faith.

# Live Lent!

I will think about the most difficult thing I face today and remember that God is with me and all will be well, no matter the outcome.

**Pray**

*God of healing and compassion, reveal to me signs of your loving presence this day. Give me eyes to see and a heart open to your amazing grace. Increase my faith and help me to put my life once again into your hands. Amen.*

## Tuesday

 **Pray**

*"God is our refuge and our strength, an ever-present help in distress. Therefore we fear not, though the earth be shaken and mountains plunge into the depths of the sea." (Psalm 46: 2-3)*

 **Read** *John 5:1-16*

**Summary:**     *"Now there is in Jerusalem at the Sheep Gate a pool called in Hebrew Bethesda, with five porticoes. In these lay a large number of ill, blind, lame, and crippled. One man was there who had been ill for thirty-eight years. When Jesus saw him lying there and knew that he had been ill for a long time, he said to him, 'Do you want to be well?' The sick man answered him, 'Sir, I have no one to put me into the pool when the water is stirred up; while I am on my way, someone else gets down there before me.' Jesus said to him, 'Rise, take up your mat, and walk.' Immediately the man became well, took up his mat, and walked." (Matthew 6: 7-8)*

*Spend two minutes in silence. Then repeat this passage from Scripture and let it speak to your heart.*

---

**Meditation**

Like the man in the gospel story who had been lying at the healing pool for thirty-eight years, we have all sorts of excuses for avoiding healing in our lives. We put up all sorts of defenses to prevent healing in our hearts. What would it look like to be a whole, healthy, spiritually free person? What healing do you need in your life? Are you willing to step out in faith and ask for it? Don't wait for your disease or your wounded spirit to bring you to death. Stand on your feet like a strong, spiritual person made whole! Become unstuck, move forward, and walk toward your Savior and your God.

# Live Lent!

I will reflect on one area of my life that needs healing and take a single step in that direction. I might call a doctor, research healthy eating, create an exercise plan, call a friend with whom I have an unresolved dispute, or seek help with financial issues.

 **Pray**

*Lord Jesus, help me name my illness or distress and bring my desire for healing and wholeness to you. Open my heart to hear you say, "Rise and live!" Amen.*

## Wednesday

 **Pray**

*"Can a mother forget her infant, be without tenderness for the child of her womb? Even should she forget, I will never forget you."* (Isaiah 49:15)

 **Read** *John 5:17-30*

**Summary:**    *"'For just as the Father raises the dead and gives life,*

---

so also does the Son give life to whomever he wishes. … Amen, amen, I say to you, whoever hears my word and believes in the one who sent me has eternal life and will not come to condemnation, but has passed from death to life.'" (John 5:21, 24)

*Spend two minutes in silence. Then repeat this passage from Scripture and let it speak to your heart.*

## Meditation

In the Old Testament, giving life is presented as a prerogative of God. In today's gospel reading Jesus claims the same authority as God the Father—the power over life and death. Sometimes we find ourselves spiritually dead. We feel unloved, and our spirit is flat. Jesus, who is the power of God, came to give us life. If you are dissatisfied with your spiritual vitality, give your life over once again to Christ, who loves you unconditionally and has the power to give you new life.

# Live Lent!

I will reach out today with an act of kindness to someone who seems to be neglected, alone, or feeling lost.

## Pray

*Loving God, you are the author of life. Thank you for your unconditional love revealed in Jesus and for never forgetting me, even when others do. Pour forth your mercy and compassion upon me, so I may see and treat each person as one of your beautiful children. Amen.*

## Thursday

## Pray

"God so loved the world that he gave his only-begotten Son, so that everyone who believes in him might have eternal life." (John 3:16)

 **Read** *John 5:31-47*

**Summary:** *"'But I have testimony greater than John's. The works that the Father gave me to accomplish, these works that I perform testify on my behalf that the Father has sent me.'"* (John 5:36)

*Spend two minutes in silence. Then repeat this passage from Scripture and let it speak to your heart.*

 **Meditation**

Frank Lloyd Wright, a famous American architect, once said, "The truth is more important than the facts." Jesus performed miracles on the Sabbath and thus was accused of violating God's law. The fact was that he did disobey the letter of the Law, but his detractors could not see past that. It didn't matter to them that Jesus healed a man who was ill for thirty-eight years and gave him the power to walk—that was beside the point. We too can become overly caught up in rules and regulations and miss the spirit of the law. The greatest rule Jesus gave us is to love God and to love our neighbor as ourselves. All other laws come second to this great commandment. Fear, insecurity, and ideology can bind us to law and shelter us from wrestling with the facts, thereby keeping us from realizing the fullness of truth in love.

# Live Lent!

I will call to mind someone whom I have written off for not living as I think that he or she should live. I will pray for that person, and ask God to show me Jesus' presence in that person's life. Then, I will add a prayer for God to help me recognize Jesus' presence more fully in my own life.

 **Pray**

*Compassionate God, give me the grace to follow your will and way. Help me to follow the spirit of your law and to always give people the benefit of the doubt. Give me the courage to wrestle with the facts and always seek the fullness of truth in love. Amen.*

---

## Friday

 **Pray**

*"The Lord is close to the brokenhearted; and those who are crushed in spirit he saves. Many are the troubles of the just man, but out of them all the Lord delivers him."* (Psalm 34:19-20)

 **Read** *John 7:1-2, 10, 25-30*

**Summary:**  *"Some of the inhabitants of Jerusalem said, 'Is he not the one they are trying to kill? And look, he is speaking openly and they say nothing to him. Could the authorities have realized that he is the Christ? But we know where he is from.'"* (John 7:25-26)

*Spend two minutes in silence. Then repeat this passage from Scripture and let it speak to your heart.*

 **Meditation**

In the scene described in today's gospel reading, Jesus is a marked man. He has infuriated both the religious and political leaders of his day, and they have threatened his life. At first Jesus did not go to Judea because he knew his life was in danger there. However, he later chose to put aside fear and go to Jerusalem for the Feast of Tabernacles and began teaching in the temple area in full view. We may not be marked men or women, but we also need courage to live and witness to our faith in secular society. We, too, have been sent by God to announce his presence to anyone who will hear us.

# Live Lent!

Today, I will pray for the many innocent Christians all over the world who risk their lives as they go to church, open their businesses each day, or walk down the street. As time allows, I will research this issue and see how I might help spread the word about today's Christian martyrs.

**Pray**

Gracious God, help me to stand firm in my faith convictions. Fill me with your courage and power, so I may share your word by the testimony of my life and the truth of my words. I pray for those who risk their lives each day for the sake of the gospel. Amen.

## Saturday

 **Pray**

"Do me justice, O Lord, because I am just, and because of the innocence that is mine. Let the malice of the wicked come to an end, but sustain the just, O searcher of heart and soul, O just God." (Psalm 7:9b-10)

 **Read** John 7:40-53

**Summary:**  "Some in the crowd who heard these words of Jesus said, 'This is truly the Prophet.' Others said, 'This is the Christ.' But others said, 'The Christ will not come from Galilee, will he? Does not Scripture say that the Christ will be of David's family and come from Bethlehem, the village where David lived?' So a division occurred in the crowd because of him. Some of them even wanted to arrest him, but no one laid hands on him." (John 7:40-44)

*Spend two minutes in silence. Then repeat this passage from the Scripture and let it speak to your heart.*

 **Meditation**

The Pharisees in today's reading claimed that the working people in town were being led astray by this false prophet from Galilee. The Pharisees were frustrated that these common people did not know the

Law or the Scriptures. If the people knew the Scriptures, they certainly would not expect that the Messiah would come from this obscure place. Nicodemus tried to speak up to encourage his fellow Pharisees to open their minds and give Jesus a hearing, but they refused. They could not get beyond Jesus being from Galilee. The Pharisees were dead wrong about the true origin and identity of Jesus. Jesus was not from Galilee, nor was he simply a prophet; he was from God. He was God.

## Live Lent!

I will recall someone I have considered being from the "wrong side of the tracks" and ask God to forgive my blindness.

 **Pray**

*Lord, free me from prejudice and judgment of others. Give me the courage to stand up and advocate for those who are harshly and rashly judged because of external circumstances. Amen.*

# Fifth Sunday of Lent

## The Raising of Lazarus

### Suggested Environment

A small table with a burning candle and a Bible opened to the gospel reading for this session. Consider decorating the table with violet, the liturgical color of the Lenten season. Place a tumbled strip of gauze on the table.

### Liturgical Readings for the Fifth Sunday of Lent

EZEKIEL 37:12-14
*God will raise believers from their graves.*

PSALM 130:1-2, 3-4, 5-6, 7-8
*God redeems us from the depths of despair.*

ROMANS 8:8-11
*Christ's Spirit dwelling within us is our life.*

JOHN 11:1-45
*Jesus raises Lazarus from the dead.*

### Focus

As for his beloved friend, Lazarus, Jesus is our resurrection and life.

---

**Opening Song** (To download, visit ocp.org/renew-music.)
"*Be Not Afraid*," Bob Dufford, SJ

 **Opening Prayer**

Form two groups, and pray alternately from Psalm 130, with everyone repeating the response:

**R. With the Lord there is mercy and fullness of redemption.**

**Side 1:** *Out of the depths I cry to you, O Lord;*
*Lord, hear my voice!*
*Let your ears be attentive*
*to my voice in supplication.*

**R. With the Lord there is mercy and fullness of redemption.**

**Side 2:** *If you, O Lord, mark iniquities,*
*Lord, who can stand?*
*But with you is forgiveness,*
*that you may be revered.*

**R. With the Lord there is mercy and fullness of redemption.**

**Side 1:** *I trust in the Lord;*
*my soul trusts in his word.*
*More than sentinels wait for the dawn,*
*let Israel wait for the Lord.*

**R. With the Lord there is mercy and fullness of redemption.**

**Side 2:** *For with the Lord is kindness*
*and with him is plenteous redemption;*
*And he will redeem Israel*
*from all their iniquities.*

**R. With the Lord there is mercy and fullness of redemption.**

 **The Gospel of the Lord**

"I am the resurrection and the life; whoever believes in me, even if he dies, will live. . . ." (John 11:25)

*Read aloud* John 11:1-45

## Reflect

*What word, phrase, or image from the scripture reading touches your heart or connects to your experience? Share with the group, and/or write your response here:*

_____

_____

_____

_____

## Old Testament Connections

Just before his death, Moses commissioned Joshua (a name equivalent to "Jesus") to lead the Israelites into the Promised Land and exhorted the people to remain faithful to the covenant God has established with them (Dt 31:1-29).

Moses' words echo in those of Jesus in the coming chapters of John's Gospel as Jesus, the new Joshua, gives his farewell address before his crucifixion and death. The author of the Book of Deuteronomy tells us that Moses was unequaled for "all the signs and wonders that the Lord sent him to perform," (Dt 34:11). Jesus offers us the definitive sign, the resurrection from the dead. Moses lives only in his words; the risen Jesus lives in his community.

Another background theme in this passage reminds us of the opening scene in this Gospel: John the Baptist proclaiming at the beginning of his ministry, "I am the voice of one crying out in the wilderness, 'Make straight the way of the Lord.'" (Jn 1:23) The evangelist John calls our attention to the words of the prophet Isaiah about the Lord coming directly to his new Jerusalem.

If this seems far afield from the raising of Lazarus from the dead, here is the basis for the connection. Lazarus was dead—completely dead for four days, to stress the metaphor. He was like Jerusalem in the days of Isaiah, a grand city totally laid waste by the Babylonians, destined to live no more. But Isaiah had the faith to tell his compatriots that God would not let this destruction stand. God would come on a straight path, levelling hills, filling in valleys, to re-establish his presence in Jerusalem. And so it happened with the rebuilding of the second Temple.

John the Baptist, as a prophet of a new era, in the mold of Moses and Isaiah, saw God returning to his people in an unexpected and unprecedented presence—that is, in the person of Jesus. This is how the community of the evangelist John understood Jesus and offered that image to us. The Temple of the evangelist's time was as dead as it was in Isaiah's time. But in this new era it was replaced, but not by another temple or another city. It was replaced by God himself in the person of Jesus. The great and singular God of Israel did not simply lead the nation back to its former glory, he came himself into the human family!

Jesus is the new Temple who gives us a new understanding of the Feast of Tabernacles. The evangelist John has also showed us, at the beginning of this Gospel, Jesus overturning the money changers' tables, a symbol of the Temple's destruction, and proclaiming that he would build the new Temple in three days.

For the community of the evangelist John, the resurrection of Lazarus was the symbol of new life. Jesus died, as we all do, "emptied himself … and becoming obedient to the point of death, even death on a cross" (Phil 2:7-8). Paul's words capture the paradox of death followed by resurrection that we are left to ponder. In this mode of thinking, death has lost its sting because eternal life begins in our lifetime and transitions into a deeper unity with the divine. Eternal life begins with the acceptance that God has come to offer his love to us in the form of Jesus, truly a human person and truly God endowed with our flesh.

*Adapted from a reflection by Martin Lang in* John: I Am the Vine, *a forthcoming part of the* RENEW Scripture Series.

## Reflect

*The sisters of Lazarus assumed that the death of their brother meant the end of their daily relationship with him. How does your faith help you deal* with the knowledge that, in this world, you will no longer see or interact with a friend or loved one who has died? Share with the group, and/or write your response here.

_____

_____

_____

_____

 ## Meditation

Bob, a generous and amiable man of deep faith, volunteered at our RENEW office with his wife, Marge, every week for many years. There was nothing Bob could not fix. When this couple joined us for prayer before an annual staff picnic, Bob—in his 80s, but still with a twinkle in his eye—shared a powerful story with us. Once, from a fishing boat off the Jersey Shore, Bob saw a man fall from another vessel in the distance. The man had been cleaning fish and, as he tried to empty the fish remains into the water, the rope attached to the bucket pulled him overboard.

The others on the fisherman's boat began to scream for help, and Bob asked his own captain to assist. The captain refused, because he had not seen the man fall. When Bob insisted, describing the accident, the captain still refused. He argued that he didn't want people to think the man fell from their boat. Bob, with a power he felt was coming from outside himself, persisted until the captain turned the board toward the spot where the man had gone overboard. There was no sign of the man—not even a ripple. The lost man's wife began to weep.

Bob cried out to the Lord for his help and mercy. He followed the rope, and he and others found the man and dragged him on board. The man lay seemingly lifeless. Bob again cried to the Lord for help. He untangled the rope, which had tightened around the man's neck, gave him chest compressions, and breathed into his mouth. Bob refused to give up. The police were now on the scene, bringing the boat to shore and assisting Bob. When all seemed to be lost, the man began to breathe, got up, and was able to walk off the boat. Bob and all who witnessed the event were astonished.

With this story, Bob testified to the power of Jesus' love and mercy that brought this man back to life, reaffirming Bob's faith not only in the resurrection of Christ but also in the possibility of God bringing new life to our own seemingly hopeless situations.

As Jesus arrives at the tomb, burdened not only with his grief but also with the deep sorrow of Mary and Martha, he is deeply moved. In his grief, Jesus first thanks God, and then he calls Lazarus forth from the tomb. Lazarus comes to life, bound by the wrappings of the burial cloth. All are astonished. And Jesus says to his friends, "Untie him and let him go free." Lazarus lets himself be unbound.

We are often bound by fear, despair, and a sense of powerlessness in the face of adversity.  Bob could have turned away from the sight of the man overboard and continued his fishing expedition. Bob chose to come to the man's aid and trust in the power and mercy of God. This God experience continued to strengthen Bob as he faced his own physical diminishment and as he prepared to transition into a "deeper unity with the divine."

We have God's power within us to free us and to free others who are bound or entangled. Lent is a good time to consider what we need to be freed from. What is binding you—making it difficult for you to breathe or what do you feel entangled in? What are the places in your life, your relationship with another person, your sense of your own value, your emotional or physical health where you are resigned to death? Do you believe that God can bring you to a place of new life?

Jesus waits for us with merciful love and tender compassion. He waits to unbind us, breathe into us a spirit of freedom, and set us on the path of life.

## Reflect

*Martha was distraught because Jesus did not arrive in time to heal her brother. Have you ever felt as if God delayed in helping you in a difficult situation? When? How was your relationship with God affected by that experience?*

_____

_____

_____

_____

*The death of a relative or acquaintance is also the death of the possibility of reconciling any differences we have had with those persons. How do you try to heal such differences while there is time? How hard is that to do? Why?*

_____

_____

_____

_____

*Jesus tells Martha that those who believe in him, even if they die, shall live; and then he asks one of the most important questions in the gospels: "Do you believe this?" How do you answer? Why do you answer as you do?*

_____

_____

_____

_____

# Live Lent!

† Identify something from which you seek release, healing or new life. Imagine that you can hold this situation in your hands—pray to Jesus to open your heart and hands and to heal you.

† See if your parish has a ministry to parishioners who recently lost a loved one. These groups help in ways such as fixing meals or running errands to help people who are grieving. Offer to volunteer with this group. If your parish doesn't have a ministry like this, see about helping to organize one.

† Spend time prayerfully reviewing your Lenten Plan, (page 8), making any adjustments that you think are needed.

**Closing Prayer**

Pray together:

*God of freedom, you loose all bonds that hold us in darkness and sin. Heal the places where our wounds and pride have kept us distant from you and one another. Free us from our tombs, O Christ. Amen.*

## Looking Ahead

To prepare for the next session, read the following:

- Matthew 26:14-27:66
- Session Six: From the Last Supper to the Crucifixion.

## *Monday*

 **Pray**

*"Even though I walk in the dark valley I fear no evil; for you are at my side...."* (Psalm 23:4)

 **Read** *John 8:1-11*

**Summary:**    "'Let the one among you who is without sin be the first to throw a stone at her.' Again he bent down and wrote on the ground. And in response, they went away one by one, beginning with the elders. So he was left alone with the woman before him. Then Jesus straightened up and said to her, 'Woman, where are they? Has no one condemned you?' She replied, 'No one, sir.' Then Jesus said, 'Neither do I condemn you. Go, and from now on do not sin any more.'" (John 8:7b-11)

*Spend two minutes in silence. Then repeat this passage from Scripture and let it speak to your heart.*

 **Meditation**

A few years ago, there was international crossfire over Iran's stoning sentence for a woman convicted of adultery. A European Union official called it barbaric. An Iranian spokesman said it was about punishing a criminal—not a human-rights issue. The woman ultimately faced another form of execution. Many are unaware of the discrimination and violence against women that still exists in many parts of the world, even our own. Some secular and religious institutions still uphold outdated attitudes toward women. Jesus challenged the establishment of his day in this respect and others, and we need to do the same.

Jesus told them, "Let the one among you who is without sin be the first to throw a stone at her," and then Jesus turned to the woman and said, "Go, and from now on do not sin any more." Pope Francis reflected on this gospel passage in a short homily: "I think even we are sometimes like these people who on the one hand want to listen to Jesus, but on the other hand, sometimes we like to stone others and condemn others. The message of Jesus is this: mercy." In a soft voice he repeated, "I say in all humility that this is the strongest message of the Lord: mercy."

# Live Lent!

I will think of someone I have judged and pray for them without judgment. I will pray for myself to become more merciful.

 **Pray**

*Compassionate God, lead me on the right path. Give me the courage to speak up for the least in our society. Help me to turn from my sinful ways and toward your gracious mercy. Amen.*

## Tuesday

 **Pray**

*"O Lord, hear my prayer, and let my cry come to you. Hide not your face from me on the day of my distress. Incline you ear to me; in the day when I call, answer me speedily." (Psalm 102:2-3)*

 **Read** *John 8:21-30*

**Summary:**  *"So Jesus said to them, 'When you lift up the Son of Man, then you will realize that I AM, and that I do nothing on my own, but I say only what the Father taught me. The one who sent me is with me. He has not left me alone, because I do what is pleasing to him.'" (John 8: 28-29)*

*Spend two minutes in silence. Then repeat this passage from Scripture and let it speak to your heart.*

 **Meditation**

In the gospel passage, Jesus tries convincing the religious leaders that he is sent from God. He tells them they will die in their sins unless they come to believe in him. Jesus points to the connection between the bronze snake being lifted up in the Book of Numbers and the way he will soon be lifted up on the cross. God used the hated symbol of Roman oppression—the cross—and turned it into a means of healing and salvation.

Look at the cross in a new way—as God's people looked at the snake in the desert. Face your sin, and look for healing. Gaze at the cross and remember the sins of injustice, cruelty, and violence endemic in our world, but have faith in God's mercy for those who seek him.

# Live Lent!

If possible, I will attend the Good Friday liturgy, rearranging my schedule as needed. If I cannot attend, I will reflect on the Stations of the Cross.

 **Pray**

*Suffering Christ, strengthen my belief in your redeeming work on the cross. Let me not turn from the evil in the world or rationalize my own sinful behavior, but look at you and live. Amen.*

## Wednesday

 **Pray**

*"Blessed are they who have kept the word with a generous heart and yield a harvest through perseverance."* (See Luke 8:15)

**Read** *John 8:31-42*

**Summary:** *"Jesus said to those Jews who believed in him, 'If you remain in my word, you will truly be my disciples, and you will know the truth, and the truth will set you free.'"* (John 8:31)

*Spend two minutes in silence. Then repeat this passage from Scripture and let it speak to your heart.*

 ## Meditation

In the gospel passage, Jesus made three promises to those who committed to obey his word, "to do the right thing": they would be his disciples; they would know the truth; and the truth would set them free. The first two promises his hearers accepted, but the third one, they resisted because it insinuated that they were not yet free. They argued with Jesus that they were the children of Abraham and never had been slaves to anyone. They were stuck on the literal meaning of slavery while Jesus reinterpreted slavery as being a slave to sin.

What are the sins that keep you from being free? What are the worries, bad habits, and attachments that may not be sinful but that keep you bound?

# Live Lent!

I will review my life and bring to the Lord my worries, bad habits, and unhealthy attachments. I will humbly face the truth of my situation, and ask God to set me free.

 ## Pray

*Jesus, you are the way, the truth, and the life. Heal me. Amen.*

**Pray**

*"If today you hear his voice, harden not your hearts."* (Psalm 95:8)

 **Read** *John 8:51-59*

**Summary:** *"Jesus said to them, 'Amen, amen, I say to you, before Abraham came to be, I AM.' So they picked up stones to throw at him; but Jesus hid and went out of the temple area."* (John 8:58-59)

*Spend two minutes in silence. Then repeat this passage from Scripture and let it speak to your heart.*

 **Meditation**

Elizabeth Barrett Browning wrote a poem describing the scene when Moses, before going to face pharaoh in Egypt, encountered God, self-described as "I AM," in the burning bush. She wrote:

> *Earth's crammed with heaven,*
> *And every common bush afire with God;*
> *But only he who sees takes off his shoes.*
> *The rest sit round it and pluck blackberries,*
> *And daub their natural faces unaware.*
> From "Aurora Leigh," vs. 61-65

Earth is crammed with heaven, and God is present in our world. It is to this created world that God sent his only son, Jesus, not to condemn the world but to save it.

# Live Lent!

I will be attentive to the presence of God in all that surrounds me today, and I will give God thanks.

**Pray**

*Jesus, you are the light of the world. Give me new eyes that I might be more aware of God's holy presence in my life this day. Amen.*

## Friday

 **Pray**

*"I love you, O Lord, my strength, O Lord, my rock, my fortress, my deliverer." (Psalm 18:2-3a)*

 **Read** *John 10:31-42*

**Summary:**   *"'If I do not perform my Father's works, do not believe me; but if I perform them, even if you do not believe me, believe the works, so that you may realize and understand that the Father is in me and I am in the Father.'" (John 10: 37-38)*

*Spend two minutes in silence. Then repeat this passage from Scripture and let it speak to your heart.*

 **Meditation**

In our gospel reading for today, Jesus continues to challenge the Jewish leaders and tries to win their hearts, but they are so stuck on their understanding of Scripture and tradition that they are closed to God's presence in Jesus' works. Jesus reminds them, "I have shown you many good works from my father. For which of these are you trying to stone me?" Could it be for Jesus' works of preaching, healing, forgiving, praising God, caring for those who are poor, or for reaching out to those on the margins of society? Many Jews listened to Jesus; they saw his good works and came to believe he was from God. But others ignored his works and couldn't get past their perception that he was blaspheming by making himself God.

# Live Lent!

I will do a work of God for someone in need today, especially someone in my family.

 **Pray**

*God of the poor and brokenhearted, give me the grace to reveal Jesus today by my loving words, patient responses, and kind action. Amen.*

## Saturday

 **Pray**

*"My dwelling shall be with them; I will be their God, and they shall be my people."* (Ezekiel 37:27)

 **Read** *John 11:45-56*

**Summary:**    *"So from that day on they planned to kill him. So Jesus no longer walked about in public... Now the Passover of the Jews was near, ... They looked for Jesus and said to one another as they were in the temple area, 'What do you think? That he will not come to the feast?'"* (John 11: 53-54a, 55a, 56)

*Spend two minutes in silence. Then repeat this passage from Scripture and let it speak to your heart.*

 **Meditation**

Since the Second Vatican Council, popes have been determined to exercise their role as pastors by having more direct contact with lay Catholics and many others. Pope Francis, beginning on the day after his election, sought to have face-to-face encounters with ordinary people. Risk is always involved when public figures step outside the ring of security; in fact, both Pope Paul VI and Pope John Paul II were the targets of assassination attempts. But modern popes have not been deterred by that risk any more than Jesus was deterred by the danger he faced.

Jesus went to the feast, and he was arrested and put to death. He had warned his followers that he would die, but also promised them that from his death would come salvation and eternal life. As you observe Holy Week, be aware of the many ways in which you can die for others by giving a part of yourself for someone who needs it.

# Live Lent!

I will work to be Christ's presence today, especially where it feels risky to me. I will be bold and reach out to others in need, even if it's as simple as holding a door open.

 **Pray**

*Lord Jesus, Savior of the world, as I prepare to walk with you during Holy Week, give me a courageous and expansive heart, ready and willing to take a risk; to give away my life each day for others. Amen.*

# Palm Sunday of the Passion of the Lord

## From the Last Supper to the Crucifixion

### Suggested Environment

A small table with a burning candle and a Bible opened to the gospel reading for this session. Consider decorating the table with red, the liturgical color for Passion Sunday. Place a cross or crucifix on the table.

### Liturgical Readings for
### Palm Sunday of the Passion of the Lord

ISAIAH 50:4-7
*I will not be put to shame for faithfulness to God.*

PSALM 22:8-9, 17-18, 19-20, 23-24
*"My God, my God, why have you abandoned me?"*

PHILIPPIANS 2:6-11
*He was obedient, even to death on a cross.*

MATTHEW 26:14-27:66
*The gentiles witnessed, "Truly, this was the Son of God."*

### Focus

We are given the Eucharist, and we must journey with Jesus to the cross.

**Opening Song** (To download, visit ocp.org/renew-music.)

*"Behold the Wood,"* Dan Schutte

 **Opening Prayer**

Form two groups , and pray alternately from Psalm 22, with everyone repeating the response:

**R. My God, my God, why have you abandoned me?**

**Side 1:**     *All who see me scoff at me;*
     *they mock me with parted lips, they wag their heads:*
     *"He relied on the Lord; let him deliver him,*
     *let him rescue him, if he loves him."*

**R. My God, my God, why have you abandoned me?**

**Side 2:**     *Indeed, many dogs surround me,*
     *a pack of evildoers closes in upon me;*
     *They have pierced my hands and my feet;*
     *I can count all my bones.*

**R. My God, my God, why have you abandoned me?**

**Side 1:**     *They divide my garments among them,*
     *and for my vesture they cast lots.*
     *But you, O Lord, be not far from me;*
     *O my help, hasten to aid me.*

**R. My God, my God, why have you abandoned me?**

**Side 2:**     *I will proclaim your name to my brethren;*
     *in the midst of the assembly I will praise you:*
     *"You who fear the Lord, praise him;*
     *all you descendants of Jacob, give glory to him;*
     *revere him, all you descendants of Israel!"*

**R. My God, my God, why have you abandoned me?**

 **The Gospel of the Lord**

Jesus is betrayed, suffers, and dies, but he leaves us the Eucharist.

*Read aloud* Matthew 26:20-32

## Reflect

*What word, phrase, or image from the scripture reading touches your heart or connects to your experience? Share with the group, or write your response here:*

_____

_____

_____

_____

## Old Testament Connections

Followers of Jesus construed the Temple priests' rejection of Jesus as a rejection of God's plan for his people. Thus God withdrew from his presence among them, leaving their enemies to conquer them (in 70 AD). This was a day of darkness rather than light as the prophet Amos said (Am 5:18). The darkness "over the whole land" at the time of Jesus' crucifixion foreshadowed this catastrophe.

Two psalms show a faithful servant of God on the verge of death at the hands of his enemies. Psalm 69 portrays the servant's sense of abandonment by all of his friends in the last moments. It also reflects the cruelties of the servant's enemies: "I looked for compassion, but there was none; for comforters, but found none. Instead, they gave me poison for my food, and for my thirst they gave me vinegar" (verses 21-22).

In Psalm 22, not only are friends and supporters absent but God himself seems to have withdrawn, as he said he would to those who did not keep the covenant. "My God, my God why have you abandoned me?" (verse 2) The servant trusted entirely in God and now, when he is being torn to pieces by his enemies, he does not feel God's presence:

"Dogs surround me, a pack of evildoers closes in on me. They have pierced my hands and my feet I can count all my bones" (verses 17-18a). Just as the psalmist had described, Jesus was mocked by the bystanders, and his garments were divided among his enemies.

In the end (verses 24-28), the abandoned servant of Psalm 22 experiences the consolation of God and proclaims to those around him that God does not forget the poor or ignore their suffering; God does not turn away but answers those who call for help.

This final vindication by God is understood to take place in the resurrection of Jesus and in the resurrection of all his servants who suffered like him in emptiness and abandonment. The resurrection of the just reflects the teaching of the prophet Ezekiel as he speaks God's words: "You shall know that I am the Lord, when I open your graves and make you come out of them, O my people," (Ez 37:13). We see this fulfilled at the moment of Jesus' death. The beginning of a new era of relationship to God occurs at that moment. We learn that God is the ultimate ruler of this world, the Lord over life and death. In the end it is God's agenda that is completed for humankind, not the will of his creatures.

*Adapted from a reflection by Martin A. Lang in* Matthew: Come Follow Me, *a forthcoming part of the* RENEW Scripture Series.

## Reflect

*Jesus knows that his journey will lead to death. While he struggles with this in the garden, he ultimately accepts that he, like the suffering servant of the psalm, must trust God to the end. Have you ever faced an experience that seemed too great to bear? What was it? How did you navigate it? What role did your faith play in that journey? Share with the group, and/or write your response here.*

_____

_____

_____

_____

 **Meditation**

I participated in World Youth Day 2016 in Krakow, Poland with 2 million enthusiastic young Catholics from around the globe. It was an experience of faith and hope that reignited my zeal for God and mission.  However, the most powerful part of my pilgrimage to Poland was a visit to Auschwitz-Birkenau, the Nazi death camp where approximately 1.1 million Jews were exterminated along with 200,000 others. I was deeply moved and disturbed as I walked the expansive and grim grounds; entered the gas chambers where men, women, and children were suffocated; crossed the railroad platform where the movement of an officer's thumb sent one to either a work camp or the death chamber; prayed at the brick wall where condemned prisoners were shot, and moved through the brick barracks displaying mounds of shoes, toothbrushes, shaving brushes, glasses, and other personal property.

The room that had the most impact on me was the one in which two tons of human hair was displayed behind glass. I could barely look at it, and my revulsion was made worse when our guide told us hair like this was used by the Nazis to make textiles and other products.

Many times the guide reminded us that what happened at Auschwitz-Birkenau didn't happen just because of a small number of monstrously evil people. It happened also because other people cooked meals, drove trains, designed and built the barracks and, worse, the ovens—people, doing ordinary jobs, who did not know or chose not to know about the horrendous genocide taking place on these grounds. I asked the guide how she could keep coming to this place. She said, "My grandfather was killed here, and I come here each day to warn people against our darkest instincts—to objectify our fellow human beings." Overwhelmed by the cruelty and evil, I entered cell block 11 where Maximilian Kolbe, a Franciscan priest, died as prisoner No. 16670 in 1941. Father Kolbe was sent to the death camp because he and other friars had organized a shelter for 3,000 Polish refuges among whom were 2,000 Jews. In his cell a lit paschal candle cast a small light on the grim surroundings—a sign of Christ's victory over

---

suffering and death. How I needed that light.

In July of 1941, a prisoner had escaped and the officers picked ten men to be starved to death as a means of discouraging others from fleeing. One of the chosen was Polish army sergeant Franciszek Gajowniczek. Because Gajowniczek had a wife and children, Father Kolbe proposed to the Nazis that he be allowed to take the sergeant's place. The Nazis agreed, and the priest and the other condemned men were consigned to a kind of dungeon. He languished there until he was near death and was finally killed with a lethal injection. A survivor, Jerzy Bielecki, declared that Father Kolbe's sacrifice was a "shock filled with hope, bringing new life and strength…it was like a powerful shaft of light in the darkness of the camp." Maximilian Kolbe was canonized in 1982.

On the Sunday before his death, Jesus rode into Jerusalem as people lined the road shouting his praises and thanking God for the miracles they had seen. By Friday they were shouting, "Give us Barabbas, we want him. Crucify Jesus, crucify him." In one short week, they turned on Jesus. Many collaborated with the Romans who stripped, beat, and hanged Jesus, the suffering servant of God, on the cross. However, darkness would not prevail, and through the sacrifice of Christ the powerful shaft of resurrection light continues to permeate the world.

Maximilian Kolbe shows us what it means to be a good and faithful servant in the worst of times and conditions. The first sign of his faithfulness was sheltering refugees; the ultimate sign, like Jesus, the suffering servant, was voluntarily giving up his life for another.

Auschwitz, like Calvary, is a grim place overshadowed by darkness that has been preserved to remind us of the worst possibilities of human behavior. It also shines light on the best possibilities by reminding us of what can happen when someone embodies Christ's saving love and mercy for the sake of the world.

## Reflect

*When you hear about the heroism of someone like Maximilian Kolbe in*

---

*circumstances that none of us are likely to endure, how can you relate it to the challenges you perceive around you in everyday life?*

_____

_____

_____

_____

*Jesus taught that there is no greater love than to lay down one's life for a friend—a belief he literally lived out for us. When has another person shown self-giving love for you? When have you done it for another?*

_____

_____

_____

_____

*There are still many "Calvarys" in the world. The story of Jesus Christ does not end with the crucifixion; the cross is a step toward the resurrection. What opportunities might be waiting for you or your parish to bring new life where there now is despair?*

_____

_____

_____

_____

# Live Lent!

✝ *Pray today for people everywhere who have been persecuted because of what they believe, where they come from, or who they are.*

✝ *Research the work of Catholic Relief Services, the official overseas relief and development agency of the United States Conference of Catholic Bishops, to see how the Catholic Church in the United States is affecting the lives of our brothers and sisters around the world (www.crs.org ). Decide how you can best support this work.*

✝ *Spend time prayerfully reviewing your Lenten Plan (page 8), making any adjustments that you think are needed.*

 **Closing Prayer**

Pray together:

*Lord Jesus, You loved us so deeply that you were willing to love us unto death, death on a cross. When we see brothers and sisters who are suffering and afflicted, let us see you, and let us respond with a love "surpassing all understanding"— your love. Amen.*

## Looking Ahead

To prepare for Easter, read John 20:1-9

## Monday

 **Pray**

*"Here is my servant whom I uphold, my chosen one with whom I am pleased. Upon whom I have put my Spirit; he shall bring forth justice to the nations." (Isaiah 42:1)*

 **Read** *John 12:1-11*

**Summary:**  *"Six days before Passover Jesus came to Bethany, where Lazarus was, whom Jesus had raised from the dead. They gave a dinner for him there, and Martha served, while Lazarus was one of those reclining at table with him. Mary took a liter of costly perfumed oil made from genuine aromatic nard and anointed the feet of Jesus and dried them with her hair; the house was filled with the fragrance of the oil." (John 12:1-3)*

*Spend two minutes in silence. Then repeat this passage from Scripture and let it speak to your heart.*

 **Meditation**

Jesus comes into the midst of our busy lives, extending the same invitation he gave long ago to the two sisters from Bethany. Jesus invites us to choose the "the better part"—a joyful life of intimacy with him that flows naturally into loving service. All of us, Marys and Marthas alike, can draw closer to Christ: deepening our prayer life, strengthening our service, and doing both with less stress, more freedom, and spontaneous joy.

# Live Lent!

I will spend at least fifteen minutes in prayerful reflection today. I will contemplate Jesus and my personal relationship with him.

**Pray**

*Loving God, help me to deepen my prayer life and strengthen my service which flow from my love for you. Free me from judging myself and others, from resentment, and from trying to be someone I am not. Restore my joy in all I do. Amen.*

## Tuesday

 **Pray**

*"In you, O Lord, I take refuge; let me never be put to shame. In your justice rescue me, and deliver me; incline your ear to me, and save me."* (Psalm 71:1-2)

 **Read** *John 13:21-33, 36-38*

**Summary:**   *"Jesus was deeply troubled and testified, 'Amen, amen, I say to you, one of you will betray me.' ... So Simon Peter nodded to him to find out whom he meant. He leaned back against Jesus' chest and said to him, 'Master, who is it?' Jesus answered, 'It is the one to whom I hand the morsel after I have dipped it.' So he dipped the morsel and took it and handed it to Judas,  son of Simon the Iscariot. After he took the morsel, Satan entered him."* (John 13:21b, 24-27a)

*Spend two minutes in silence. Then repeat this passage from Scripture and let it speak to your heart.*

 **Meditation**

The difference between Peter and Judas is that Judas gave up on God's mercy. In contrast, Peter, who denied Christ three times, clung to faith. Peter had the capacity to experience God's mercy more than once. Judas could not move past his betrayal. No one is beyond redemption

— not Peter, not Judas, not anyone. Pope Francis emphasized this shortly after his election. In one of his first messages, the pope said: "The Lord never tires of forgiving us—never! We are the ones who get tired of asking forgiveness."

## Live Lent!

I will search my heart for any unforgiven wrong that I have done or another has done to me. I will ask God to forgive me and to bless me with the courage to forgive myself and others.

 **Pray**

*God of mercy and compassion, let me never tire of asking you for forgiveness. Pour your inexhaustible love upon me so my heart might be large enough to forgive those who hurt me. Renew my hope and cast out any despair that lingers in my spirit. Amen.*

## Wednesday

 **Pray**

*"I will praise the name of God in song, and I will glorify him with thanksgiving: ... For the Lord hears the poor, and his own who are in bonds he spurns not."* (Psalm 69:31,34)

 **Read** *Matthew 26:14-25*

**Summary:**     *"On the first day of the Feast of Unleavened Bread, the disciples approached Jesus and said, 'Where do you want us to prepare for you to eat the Passover?' He said, 'Go into the city to a certain man and tell him, The teacher says, 'My appointed time draws near; in your house I shall celebrate the Passover with my disciples.' The disciples then did as Jesus had ordered, and prepared the Passover."* (Matthew 26:17-19)

*Spend two minutes in silence. Then repeat this passage from Scripture and let it speak to your heart.*

 **Meditation**

Today is the last official day of Lent. Tomorrow, at sundown we begin the great "Three Days" or the Easter Triduum—which stretches from sundown on Holy Thursday through sundown on Easter Sunday. The Triduum liturgies include several major services and can be properly understood as one continuous act of worship commemorating the passion, death, and resurrection of Jesus, so that we mark our own dying and rising of the past year. In today's gospel passage, we read about the beginning of preparations for the final events of Jesus' life on earth. Jesus instructed the disciples to go to Jerusalem and get ready for the Passover meal. They immediately and willingly obeyed Jesus. They found an appropriate room in Jerusalem, removed any items that contained leavening, bought a lamb and had it ritually slaughtered, and made final preparations for an intimate Passover dinner with Jesus and his closest friends.

# Live Lent!

Today and tomorrow are important days. I will prepare generously and freely my heart, mind, and home for the celebration of Easter.

 **Pray**

*Loving God, lead me into these holy days with Christ with an open heart and seeking spirit. Give me a new heart and a new spirit as I enter more fully into the life, death, and resurrection of your Son, Jesus. Amen.*

## Holy Thursday

 **Pray**

*"I give you a new commandment, says the Lord: love one another as*

*I have loved you."* (John 13:34 )

 **Read** *John 13:1-15*

**Summary:**   *"So when he had washed their feet and put his
garments back on and reclined at table again, he said
to them, 'Do you realize what I have done for you?
You call me 'teacher' and 'master,' and rightly so, for
indeed I am. If I, therefore, the master and teacher,
have washed your feet, you ought to wash one
another's feet. I have given you a model to follow, so
that as I have done for you, you should also do.'"* (John
13: 12-15)

*Spend two minutes in silence. Then repeat this passage from Scripture and
let it speak to your heart.*

 **Meditation**

The unbounded and unexpected love of Jesus bends before us, washes
us clean, and urges us to treat each other—especially the least among
us—with the same love. This day reminds us that the gospel is a life to
be lived and not just an ideal to be contemplated. Jesus sends us; will
you go?

# Live Lent!

If possible tonight, I will attend the Holy Thursday liturgy, the first
sacred service of the Triduum. If I am unable to attend Holy Thursday
Mass, I will an act of service for a person in need.

 **Pray**

*Lord Jesus, send forth your cleansing and healing love upon my
entire being. Give me the grace to bow down before my sisters and
brothers and imitate your love in humble service. Amen.*

**Pray**

*"But he was pierced for our offenses, crushed for our sins; upon him was the chastisement that makes us whole, by his stripes we were healed." (Isaiah 53:5 )*

 **Read** *John 18:1-19:42*

**Summary:**     *"Now Simon Peter was standing there keeping warm. And they said to him, 'You are not one of his disciples, are you?' He denied it and said, 'I am not.' One of the slaves of the high priest, a relative of the one whose ear Peter had cut off, said, 'Didn't I see you in the garden with him?' Again Peter denied it. And immediately the cock crowed." (John 18:25-27)*

*Spend two minutes in silence. Then repeat this passage from Scripture and let it speak to your heart.*

 **Meditation**

Today we remember that we are not alone on our journey through the sufferings of this life and that our journey is never without meaning and purpose. No matter how many times we lose our footing under the weight of our crosses, God always responds with mercy and sends a "Simon" to catch us, set us on our feet, and place us on the path of life.

# Live Lent!

I will reflect on the mercy of God in my life and recall a "Simon" who recently helped me carry my cross.

 **Pray**

*Merciful Lord, I put my life into your hands. Amen.*

**Pray**

"Alleluia, alleluia, alleluia. The stone the builders rejected has become the cornerstone. By the Lord has this been done; it is wonderful in our eyes." (Psalm 118:22-23)

 **Read** *Matthew 28:1-10*

**Summary:** "After the sabbath, as the first day of the week was dawning, Mary Magdalene and the other Mary came to see the tomb. And behold, there was a great earthquake; for an angel of the Lord descended from heaven, approached, rolled back the stone, and sat upon it. His appearance was like lightning and his clothing was white as snow. ... Then the angel said to the women in reply, 'Do not be afraid! I know that you are seeking Jesus the crucified. He is not here, for he has been raised just as he said.'" (Matthew 28:1-3, 5-6a)

Spend two minutes in silence. Then repeat this passage from Scripture and let it speak to your heart.

## Meditation

Mary Magdalene and the other Mary came to the tomb that Sunday morning filled with grief and expecting only death. A sudden earthquake shook them out of their sorrow and awoke them to an angel announcing good news, assuring them: "Do not be afraid. Jesus is alive!" Like the women disciples at the tomb, we are scarred by our Good Friday stories of struggle and suffering. But we also give witness to the many kinds of resurrection experiences that are just as real in our lives.

We are an Easter people called to embrace the cross and to announce the hope of the resurrection because the tomb is empty, Jesus is alive, and he is among us.

# Live Lent!

I will name and share with someone today a resurrection happening of new life that keeps hope alive for me.

# Easter Sunday

## Pray

*"The Lord is truly risen, alleluia. To him be glory and power for all the ages of eternity, alleluia, alleluia."* Entrance Antiphon, Easter Sunday, Mass During the Day

**Read** *John 20: 1-9*

**Summary:**    *"Then the other disciple also went in, the one who had arrived at the tomb first, and he saw and believed."* (John 20:8)

## Celebrate!

Share this table prayer with those you will eat with today.
Pray together:

> *Christ has risen! Alleluia!*
> *Loving God, you who create all things*
> *and generously give us all we need,*
> *we praise you and thank you for being present with us now*
> *as we celebrate the resurrection of Jesus Christ, your Son.*
>
> *Thank you for accompanying us on our Lenten journey;*
> *please be with us during this Easter season, and always,*
> *as we strive to live as disciples of your Son.*
>
> *May the breaking of bread, today and every day,*
> *remind us of the Bread of Life, Jesus Christ,*
> *who died to atone for our sins*
> *and rose again so that we, too, may rise*
> *and live in your presence forever.*
>
> *O God, bless this food and we who share it,*
> *and be with those who cannot share it with us.*

We ask this in the name of the same Jesus Christ, who lives and reigns with you and the Holy Spirit, one God, forever and ever. Amen.

Alleluia! Christ has risen!

## APPENDIX

There are two solemnities and one feast that can fall during Lent. When they fall on Lenten weekdays, they are celebrated in place of the liturgy for those days. Meditations for these three days are included in this appendix. Check the liturgical calendar; in some jurisdictions, the dates on which these celebrations are held may be changed.

## Feast of the Chair of St. Peter

### FEBRUARY 22

 **Pray**

*"Even though I walk in the dark valley I fear no evil; for you are at my side with your rod and your staff that give me courage."* (Psalm 23:4)

 **Read** Matthew 16:13-19

**Summary:**    *"'Who do people say that the Son of Man is?' They replied, 'Some say John the Baptist, others Elijah, still others Jeremiah or one of the prophets.' He said to them, 'But who do you say that I am?' Simon Peter said in reply, 'You are the Christ, the Son of the living God.'"* (Matthew 16:13b-16)

*Spend two minutes in silence. Then repeat this passage from Scripture, and let it speak to your heart.*

 **Meditation**

Visiting the Basilica of St. Peter in Rome, especially for the first time, can be overwhelming. The sheer size of the structure—one of the largest churches in the world—the vaulted ceilings, the soaring dome, and the multitude of altars and heroic monuments can be difficult to absorb. Soaring in the apse of the church is the extraordinary monument designed by Gian Lorenzo Bernini and completed in 1666. The centerpiece of this altar is a gilt bronze reliquary in the shape of a chair; within is an actual wooden chair, traditionally venerated as the chair used by Peter, the chief of the apostles and the first bishop of Rome. This chair consists of several parts, including some that may date to the ninth century.

The Church has set aside this day—even when it falls during Lent—in order to reflect on that chair, not as an important object in itself but as a symbol of the unity that Jesus wanted for his followers. That unity is grounded in our shared faith in Jesus as the Son of God and the savior of the world, in our mutual commitment to live in keeping with his Gospel of love, and our identification with each other as members of his body, the Church. Whenever we sin, either by an overt act or by neglect, we harm the Body of Christ and undermine the unity Jesus prayed for. By contrast, as we refresh our relationship with God during Lent, we contribute new vitality to the life of the whole Church.

## Live Lent!

Today, I will pray the Nicene Creed, reflecting after each phrase how my faith in the teachings of the Church unite me with Catholic men and women around the world and across time.

 **Pray**

*Lord Jesus Christ, you prayed that your followers might be one as you and the Father are one. May I be an instrument of the unity you desire by remaining faithful to your Gospel and by witnessing to it through a life of service to others. Amen.*

# Solemnity of St. Joseph, Husband of Mary

 **Pray**

*"The promises of the Lord I will sing forever, through all generations my mouth shall proclaim your faithfulness." (Psalm 89:2)*

 **Read** *Matthew 1:16; 18-21; 24a*

**Summary:**  "(S)uch was his intention when, behold,the angel of the Lord appeared to him in a dream and said 'Joseph, son of David, do not be afraid to take Mary your wife into your home. For it is through the Holy Spirit that this child has been conceived in her. She will bear a son and you are to name him Jesus because he will save his people from their sins.'" (Matthew 1:20-21;24)

*Spend two minutes in silence. Then repeat this passage from Scripture and let it speak to your heart.*

 **Meditation**

The convent where I now live was previously home to a community of the Sisters of St. Joseph. We Dominicans moved in and quickly began to make the convent our home by putting up pictures of our Dominican saints. But one of the pictures the sisters left behind, and we left hanging, is a touching yet unusual picture of a young St. Joseph, painted as an ordinary man of his day, tenderly holding the baby Jesus. When visitors notice the picture they often ask, "Who is that?"

Joseph, usually in the background of the nativity story, stands at the beginning of Matthew's Gospel as a model of discipleship. He finds himself in a moral dilemma: he wants to show mercy to Mary and not expose her presumed disgrace, and yet he must obey the Jewish Law by not accepting what might appear to be adultery. His difficult inner deliberations are cut short by divine intervention. An angel appears to Joseph in a dream and asks him to set aside his previous understanding of God's will and to marry Mary, a pregnant woman. Sometimes we find ourselves in a moral dilemma—forced to choose between condemnation or mercy. Through Joseph's mercy and his obedience to the voice of God, Jesus, "God with Us," had a home among us.

## Live Lent!

During my lifetime have I judged someone harshly, even cut them out of my life because of a moral failing? I ask God for mercy.

 **Pray**

*Compassionate God, help me to be just and merciful. Open my ears to hear your voice and act on your Word with love. Amen.*

## Solemnity of the Annunciation of the Lord

 **Pray**

*"Here am I, Lord; I come to do your will." (Psalm 40: 8a,9a)*

 **Read** *Luke 1:26-38*

**Summary:**    *"And coming to her, he said, 'Hail, full of grace! The Lord is with you.' But she was greatly troubled at what was said and pondered what sort of greeting this might be. Then the angel said to her, 'Do not be afraid, Mary, for you have found favor with God. Behold, you will conceive in your womb and bear a son, and you shall name him Jesus.'" (Luke 1:28-31)*

*Spend two minutes in silence. Then repeat this passage from Scripture and let it speak to your heart.*

 **Meditation**

I visited the Philadelphia Museum of Art to view and pray with the painting "The Annunciation" by Henry Ossawa Tanner. Tanner, an African-American artist, painted this scene in 1898 after visiting the

Holy Land. Many traditional European paintings of this biblical scene depict Mary with a European face, wearing fancy blue robes and seated on a throne in a cathedral or palace. In contrast, Tanner paints Mary with authenticity and simplicity. He portrays her as a teenage girl, with olive skin, dressed in peasant clothes, sitting on a rumpled bed, and in a simple room. For today's Solemnity of the Annunciation, I am drawn to the pottery vessels in the corners of the painting. They represent Mary who will soon become the vessel of Jesus, the son of God and Mary.

As the painting depicts, Mary, awakened from her sleep by a divine encounter, is understandably a bit troubled and anxious, but she freely accepts the grace given to her as she responds to God's messenger, "May it be done to me according to your word." (Lk 1:38) Mary, like those pottery vessels, waits to be filled. She opens herself to God's grace, and great things happen.

## Live Lent!

Google Henry Ossawa Tanner's painting "The Annunciation," or ask someone to do it for you. Quietly reflect on the painting and ask God to speak to you through the image.

 **Pray**

*Come, O Lord. Fashion me into a vessel of your love and mercy. Help me, like Mary, to surrender my life into your hands and to live each day with amazing grace. Amen.*

## About the Author

Sr. Theresa Rickard, President and Executive director of RENEW International, is a Dominican Sister of Blauvelt, New York. She holds a Doctor of Ministry in Preaching Degree from Aquinas Institute of Theology in St. Louis, Missouri. Additionally, she earned a Master of Divinity Degree at Union Theological Seminary in New York City and a Master of Arts Degree in Religion and Religious Education at Fordham University, New York.

Sr. Terry is a national speaker, preacher, and author. She has written two Advent and Lent Devotionals in the Living Gospel series published by Ave Maria Press. She is also a contributing author to Preaching in the Sunday Assembly and We Preach Christ Crucified, published by Liturgical Press. Sister Terry is a regular contributor to the RENEW International blog under the title "God in the Stuff of Life," and you can follow her on Twitter at @SrTerryRickard.

Before joining the RENEW staff she ministered in two parishes in the South Bronx and was the Director of Vocation and Formation Ministry for her Dominican congregation. She also was a member of the Archdiocese of New York Parish Mission Team.

## Presenting RENEW International

The RENEW process, both parish-based and diocese-wide, was developed and implemented in the Archdiocese of Newark, New Jersey. Its success there led other dioceses, in the United States and in other countries, to bring RENEW to 25 million people in over 160 dioceses in the United States and 24 countries throughout the world.

Over more than four decades, RENEW International has grown from its original single RENEW process. Materials and training have been inculturated and made available in over 40 languages. We have added specific pastoral outreach to campuses and to young adults in their 20s and 30s. We have incorporated prison ministry, and provided resources for the visually impaired.

The very core of all of these processes remains the same: to help people become better hearers and doers of the Word of God. We do this by encouraging and supporting the formation of small communities that gather prayerfully to reflect on and share the Word of God, to make better connections between faith and life, and to live their faith more concretely in family, work, and community life.

As a not-for-profit organization, we sustain our pastoral outreach in part from the sales of our publications and resources and stipends for services we provide to parishes and dioceses. However, our priority is always to serve all parishes who desire to renew their faith and build the Church, regardless of their economic situation. We have been able to fulfill this mission not only in the inner-city and rural areas in the United States, but also in the developing world, especially Latin America and Africa, thanks to donations and charitable funding.

As you meet in your small group, we invite you to take a few moments to imagine the great invisible network of others, here in the United States and on the other continents. They gather, as you do, in small Christian communities, around the Word of God present in the Scripture, striving to hear and act upon that Word. Keep them in your prayer: a prayer of thanksgiving for the many graces we have experienced; a prayer that the Spirit will guide all of us as we Live Lent!

## The Structure and Flow of a Session

A faith-sharing session typically lasts about 90 minutes. The following outline for your weekly small-group meetings suggests how your time might be allocated in order to keep the group moving smoothly from one element to the next. The time frame described here is based on the assumption that participants have read the session beforehand and considered their responses to the sharing questions, making notes in the spaces provided. Of course, the group leader may adjust the timing according to the dynamics of a particular session.

More detailed suggestions for the leader are included in *Essentials for Small Group Leaders* and *Leading Prayer in Small Groups,* both available from RENEW International. For details, visit www.renewintl.org.

## Introductions · 5 minutes

If the group has not met before, if participants do not know each other, or if someone new has joined, an opportunity to get acquainted is important. People share most easily when they feel comfortable and accepted in a group.

## Focus · 5 minutes

Read the focus to call to mind the central theme of the session.

## Opening Song · 5 minutes

Play a song recommended for the session or a song of your own choosing.

## Opening Prayer · 5 minutes

A few moments of silence should precede the prayer, which is always at the heart of gatherings of Christians.

## Gospel Reading and Reflection · 20 minutes

A member of the group proclaims the Gospel. After a few minutes of silent reflection, the leader asks if anyone would like to share on the passage.

## Old Testament Connection and Reflection • 20 minutes

Members of the group take a few minutes to review the Old Testament Connection, or a member of the group may read it aloud; then those who wish share their responses to the question. This section is not a discussion of the Old Testament reading for the day's Mass, but rather a reflection on the background in Hebrew Scriptures for the gospel reading of the day.

## Meditation • 25 minutes

Members of the group take a few minutes to review the Meditation, or a member of the group may read it aloud. Members review or consider their answers to the questions; then they share their responses to one or more of the questions.

## Closing Prayer • 5 minutes

---

Songs are suggested for the moments of prayer at the opening of each small-group Sunday session. Music selections for Live Lent! are provided by our partners at OCP. The music is available as individual songs or as a nine-song digital album or "virtual CD." The individual songs and the digital album are available for purchase through RENEW International at ocp.org/renew-music

# Looking for more resources?

Don't lose the great momentum of your group.

Check out the following pages, or go to **www.renewintl.org/estore**
to find the perfect book to continue your small group.

Use the promo code **BLIV10** to get **10% OFF** any purchase.*

## Check out what's new!

See the latest RENEW books, apps and other resources at
**www.pages.renewintl.org/newresources**

*Does not apply to already reduced member prices. Cannot be used with any other offer.

## from RENEW International

## *Live Lent!* Year A, B, C

Continue your Lenten journey with the other titles in this
series for lectionary years B and C.

All three titles are written by RENEW's own Sister Terry
Rickard. *Live Lent!* will help you make the most of this
season of preparation and spiritual renewal.

- Gather weekly in small groups
- Get inspired by the Sunday Gospel readings
- Explore Old Testament insights
- Reflect and pray **each day of the week**
- Take action in everyday life

## *Advent Awakenings*

Advent is a time of spiritual anticipation amidst the
often distracting preparations for Christmas. Stay
focused on the significance of this season with *Advent
Awakenings*, a four-session faith-sharing experience
grounded in the Sunday gospel readings.

The *Advent Awakening* series is based on the
three-year cycle of the *Lectionary*. Each book contains four sessions
corresponding with the four Sundays of Advent and presents themes drawn
from the Sunday gospel readings, plus enriching devotions for family use.
Appropriate for seasonal groups, small Christian communities, and individual
reflection and prayer.

**Year A: Trust the Lord:** Urges participants to have confidence that God's
challenging call is the true way to prepare for union with Christ.

**Year B: Take the Time:** Encourages participants to prepare for Jesus' coming
by setting aside everyday busyness and become more deeply aware of God's
beckoning.

**Year C: Say Yes to God:** Prompts participants to accept the invitation of Jesus'
coming by reflecting on how to be more open to his presence in their lives.

Also available as an eBook!

**For more information visit www.renewintl.org/seasonal**

# RENEW Small-Group Leader Series

## Essentials for Small-Group Leaders

This book offers a comprehensive collection of pastoral insights and practical suggestions to help leaders guide their small groups in a way that nourishes spiritual growth. Culled from RENEW International's more than four decades of experience in pioneering and promoting small Christian communities, this book overflows with simple but effective ideas and strategies that will enhance the way these groups reflect on and respond to the Gospel.

## Leading Prayer in Small Groups

Have you ever been asked to lead prayer for your church group, council, or committee? RENEW International has developed a helpful resource called *Leading Prayer in Small Groups* to encourage you in leading fruitful group prayer experiences with confidence. *Leading Prayer in Small Groups* emphasizes the importance of group prayer for church groups of every kind and provides insight into why we pray. It also explains the role, qualities, and duties of a leader of prayer. Readers are guided through the stages of preparing group prayer and the process of effectively leading prayer for a group.

**Visit www.renewintl.org/leaders to learn more or to order.**

# RENEW Scripture Series

### Luke: My Spirit Rejoices!

*Luke: My Spirit Rejoices!* is the first book in the *RENEW Scripture Series*. Written by scripture scholar Martin Lang, this faith-sharing book engages readers with the entire Gospel and includes reflections on the content of the Gospel, the human behavior illuminated in Luke's work, and the Old Testament background for each passage. Sharing questions and opportunities to apply the gospel message to daily life make this a perfect resource for small Christian communities. Can be used individually or in a group.

### Matthew: Come Follow Me

The Gospel of Matthew is the first book in the New Testament, a distinction that reflects the high value the Church has placed on this Gospel for nearly two thousand years. *Matthew: Come Follow Me* explores this unique account of the ministry, passion, and glorification of Jesus. Written by scripture scholar Martin Lang, each chapter includes reflections on the Gospel plus sharing questions and examples of how the teaching of Jesus may apply to our everyday lives. This is a perfect resource for small groups, for personal reflection, or for homily preparation.

**For more information go to www.renewintl.org/scripture**

## PRAYERTIME Cycle A, B, C: Faith-Sharing Reflections on the Sunday Gospels

This faith-sharing resource responds to the U.S. Bishops' suggestion that "every parish meeting can begin with the reading of the upcoming Sunday's Gospel, followed by a time of reflection and faith sharing."

With each Sunday's Gospel as a focus, *PRAYERTIME* proposes meaningful reflections, focused faith-sharing questions, related questions for consideration, and prayers as a source of spiritual nourishment and inspiration.

Use *PRAYERTIME* any time of year, whenever the small community needs. It is also ideal for beginning meetings of the pastoral council, staff, and other parish groups. The themes can also be read personally as a way to prepare for Sunday Mass.

This invaluable resource is also available in Spanish:
***OREMOS Ciclo A, B, C: Reflexiones sobre los Evangelios Domincales para Compartir la Fe***

# *Spirituality for Everyday Life*
## with Ronald Rolheiser

This series is based on books by Ronald Rolheiser, OMI: *The Shattered Lantern, The Holy Longing,* and *Sacred Fire.* The RENEW series employs Fr. Rolheiser's insights to explore the phases of discipleship and what it means to be a disciple of Christ in today's world.

### *Longing for the Holy*

*Longing for the Holy* is for those who want to enrich their sense of the presence of God. Designed for either a small group faith-sharing experience or personal reflection, this book explores the implications of the central mysteries of faith– the Incarnation, the Eucharist, and the Paschal Mystery – for spirituality. Attending to the cultural challenges that keep us from realizing our true desire, it considers the important themes of church community, justice, sexuality, the practices of the spiritual life, and being a mystic of the everyday.

### *Living in the Sacred*

*Living in the Sacred* is a follow-up faith-sharing resource for *Longing for the Holy* and is based on Ronald Rolheiser's *Sacred Fire. Living in the Sacred* takes participants on a deeper spiritual journey, exploring the second stage of discipleship: "Giving your life away." Having moved through the "getting your life together" stage, participants have made life commitments in marriage or other relationships, raising children, caring for sick or elderly relatives, careers, communities, etc. *Living in the Sacred* is about how we stay true to these commitments as disciples of Christ.

**For more information visit www.renewintl.org/spirituality**

# Balancing Faith & Work: The Dynamic Leader

*Balancing Faith & Work* is designed to help professionals and business leaders bring their personal and professional lives into deeper harmony with their values.

This resource is rooted in the spiritual disciplines of St. Ignatius, the founder of the Society of Jesus, the Jesuits, and draws on modern leadership insights to prompt meaningful thought and conversation.

Perfect for small-group discussion and personal reflection.

# What, Me Holy?

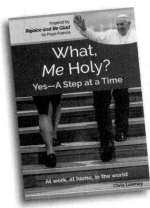

In his exhortation *Rejoice and Be Glad*, Pope Francis calls all Catholics to live a life of holiness. But what does holiness mean? Isn't holiness for heroes and martyrs? How do we answer that call in our work, in our communities, in the day-to-day encounters of our busy lives? Renowned author Chris Lowney helps unpack Pope Francis' words, inviting us to re-examine our ideas about holiness and how we answer the call to live a holy life. In twelve faith-sharing sessions, with down-to-earth, concrete examples, he opens our eyes to the everyday things we already do and those we can begin to do to lead us on a journey to holiness.

# Creation at the Crossroads:
## A Small-Group Resource based on Pope Francis' "On Care for Our Common Home (Laudato Si')"

*Creation at the Crossroads* offers twelve faith-sharing sessions that respond to Pope Francis' call to action in his encyclical on ecology, *Laudato Si'*. Participants will internalize, and set as a priority in their lives, the Church's teaching on the care of creation and the impact of environmental change on the poor and vulnerable with this small-group resource.

Through Scripture, prayer, reflections, faith-sharing questions, and practical ideas for protecting and caring for the environment and people, this resource will move Catholics to faith-based action. Ideal for use in parishes, small groups, and campus ministries.

**For more information go to www.renewintl.org/renewearth**

# Connect with us!

Now it's easier than ever to connect with the RENEW International community for daily spiritual insights and updates.

 www.facebook.com/RENEWIntl

 blog.renewintl.org

 @RENEWIntl

 YouTube.com/user/RENEWInternational

Photo by Eric Clayton/CRS

**CRS RICE BOWL**
CATHOLIC RELIEF SERVICES

CRS Rice Bowl has been inspiring families to put their faith into action to help communities around the world for 45 years.

Participate with your family by visiting **crsricebowl.org.**